Fuyuhiko Sekido

Izumi Osada

Yuichi Nishijima

TOEIC® L&R Test: Active Training

Asahi Press

音声再生アプリ「リスニング・トレーナー」を使った音声ダウンロード

朝日出版社開発のアプリ、「リスニング・トレーナー（リストレ）」を使えば、教科書の音声をスマホ、タブレットに簡単にダウンロードできます。どうぞご活用ください。

◉ アプリ【リスニング・トレーナー】の使い方

《アプリのダウンロード》

App Store または Google Play から「リスニング・トレーナー」のアプリ（無料）をダウンロード

App Storeはこちら▶

Google Playはこちら▶

《アプリの使い方》

① アプリを開き「コンテンツを追加」をタップ
② 画面上部に【15668】を入力しDoneをタップ

音声ストリーミング配信 》》》

この教科書の音声は、右記ウェブサイトにて無料で配信しています。

https://text.asahipress.com/free/english/

はしがき

　本書はTOEIC L&Rテストの対策を目指したテキストです。しかし、問題だけをただひたすらやるというタイプのものではありません。学習者であるみなさん一人一人がちゃんと各自の目標を設定し、それを継続的学習でクリア出来るような仕掛けを施してあります。特にUnit 1ではそうしたことを明確に出来るようにしてあります。よって、授業の中だけでなく、授業が終わった後も継続的に学習していってください。具体的には、特にリスニングにおいては、放送された音声のスクリプトもそれぞれのUnitにつけてありますので、音読したり、聞き取れなかった単語を確認出来たりします。ぜひ積極的に活用してください。リーディングでは、テストにおいては書き込みがルールとして禁止になってはいるものの、学習のときはいろいろマークしたり、線を引いて理解をしたい諸君もいると思います。テキストにそのまま書き込んでしまうと復習の際に再度問題にチャレンジすることが出来なくなってしまいますので、それを避けるために別途PDFで問題文用紙を用意してあります。必要に応じてそれらをダウンロードし、活用してください。(PDFファイルは以下のURLにあります。)

https://text.asahipress.com/free/dlenglish/toeicactive/

　なお、言うまでもなくこのテキストは大学の授業で用いられることを前提に作られています。ひとりで学べる部分もありますが、クラスメイトと積極的に意見交換や学びあいが出来るようにもしてあります。もちろん、そうしたことは担当されている先生の指示に従ってのことになりますが、ぜひクラスメイトとコミュニケーションをしながら、目標をクリアしたいという気持ちを忘れずに学んでいってほしいと思います (TOEICのCはCommunicationですから!)。また、そうしたコミュニケーションを促進するための手法として、コーチングというものがあります。「本書の使い方」の最後にそれを簡潔に説明しておきましたので、参考にしてください。

みなさんが本書をきっかけにTOEIC L&Rテストの学習に積極的に取り組み、それぞれの目標スコアをクリア出来ることを願っています。

2021年　執筆者代表　関戸冬彦

本書の使い方

　本書はUnit 1、8、15を除き、各Unitは同じ構成になっており、基本的にそれに沿って進行していきます。

学習ポイント 1

今日学習するリスニングのパートの説明がなされています。どういう特徴があるのか、どういうタイプの設問があるのか、理解しましょう。また、問題に臨む際のポイントも解説してありますので、実際に問題をやる時の参考にしてください。

学習ポイント 2

リスニングの問題です。音声を聞きながら、問題を解いてみましょう。

学習ポイント 3

先にやった問題のスクリプトが掲載されています。ちゃんと聞き取れていたかどうか、スクリプトを読むことで確認してみてください。また、間違えやすいポイント、ひっかけのポイントなどは線を引いたりしてチェックしておくと学びが定着します。また、リスニングの強化するためのトレーニングとして、音読なども授業内外で行ってください。

学習ポイント 4

今日学習するリーディングのパートの説明がなされています。どういうタイプの設問があるのか理解しましょう。どういう特徴があるのか、どういうタイプの設問があるのか、理解しましょう。また、問題に臨む際のポイントも解説してありますので、実際に問題をやる時の参考にしてください。

学習ポイント 5

リーディングの問題です。解答の制限時間を意識しながら、問題を解いてみましょう。

学習ポイント 6

リーディング問題の分析ページです。何を基準に、どういう理由からその選択肢を選んだのかをはっきりさせることで、正解の根拠や誤答を選んでしまった要因を分析します。本文に直接書き込みをしたい場合は、はしがきにも書きましたように、これらのページのPDFファイルを有効に活用してください。

なお、Unit 2からUnit 7で全パートを網羅してあり、Unit 9からUnit 14もそれと同じ順序で全パートを扱っています。つまり、同じ学習課程を2度辿ることによって、それぞれのパートにおける大切なことを定着させるねらいがあります。

また、Unit 8と15はリスニング25問、リーディング25問、合計50問のクォーター模試

になっています。問題は先生から配布されますので、テキスト付属のマークシートを使ってやってみてください。時間は30分です。模試終了後は、答え合わせをした後で出来たところ、出来なかったところ、得意／不得意なパートや問題を確認し、自己分析してみましょう。それを基に、さらに深く学習していけるはずです。

さて、はしがきにも記したコーチングをここで説明します。コーチングとは、「人が本来もっている能力が最大限に引き出され、可能性が開花することを目的とする、理論的・標準的・体系的なコミュニケーションのプロセス」です。その狙いは「学生に主体的な行動をうながし、目標・目的に向かって前進させること」にあります。本テキストにおいてはTOEIC L&Rテストの学習、スコアアップが主たる目的ですが、それを可能にするためにはこのテキストをただ学ぶ、あるいは答え合わせをするだけでは不十分で、自ら積極的にテキストとTOEIC、そして英語学習に取り組む必要があります。それを可能にするのは誰でもない、みなさん学習者自身です。つまり、コーチングはみなさんの積極性、動機を高めるための手段になるのです。よって本テキストでは、Unitが終わるごとにその日の授業の振り返りと、授業後の学習目標を書く欄があります。それを基に、ペアでお互いコーチングをして、ポジティブな気持ちで終えるようにしましょう。

コーチングをするためには以下の3つのことを覚えておいて下さい。

1　相手が主役であり、相手の中に答えがある
2　相手の可能性は無限であり、相手の未来を信じる
3　相手の成長・成功を信じ、その実現へ向けて伴走する

本テキストで言えば、クラスメイトがTOEIC L&Rテストで目標とするスコアが取れることを信じ、その可能性を同じクラスメイトである「あなた」が引き出してあげるということです。そのためにすることは以下の3つです。

1　相手のための質問

具体的には、相手に対して気づきをもたらす質問、行動をうながす質問、変化をうながす質問をしましょう。

2　傾聴

相手の話を遮らず最後まで聴き、アイコンタクトやうなづき、あいづちをしましょう。

3　承認

ネガティブな事は言わず、相手の具体的な行動、事実を取り上げて認めてあげましょう。

これらの発想の根本には「人は気がつくと行動を起こし、行動を起こすと変化する」があります。ぜひこのテキストとコーチングを通じて、みなさん自身のTOEIC学習に変化を起こしてください!

＊コーチングについては北海学園大学経営学部教授、菅原秀幸氏から示唆を得ました。

目次

TOEIC®
L&R Test:
Active
Training

Unit 1　What is TOEIC?

最初のUnitではまずTOEICとはどういうテストなのかを学びましょう。以下、情報を一部（　　　）に入れていますので、知っている人は知っている情報を、知らない人、もしくは知らない部分はペアで、グループで共有して埋めてみましょう。それでもわからないところはとりあえずカンで埋めてみてください。

TOEIC (Test of English for International Communication) はETS (Educational Testing Service) というアメリカの非営利テスト開発機関によって作成されているテストです。

　　　テスト時間は（　　　）時間で、リスニングが（　　　）分、リーディングが（　　　）分です。

　　　問題数はリスニング、リーディング共に（　　　）問の合計（　　　）問です。なお、リスニングはPart 1〜4、リーディングはPart 5〜7です。

　　　点数はリスニング、リーディングそれぞれ（　　　）が最高得点で、総点としては（　　　）点から（　　　）点の幅でスコアが出ます。

どうでしょうか？ここまで何か言葉や数字を入れてみましたか？答え合わせは、以下のURLから出来ます。あるいはGoogleでTOEICと検索すればすぐに見つかります。

IIBC TOEIC公式サイト　https://www.iibc-global.org/toeic.html

ちなみに、TOEFLとはどう違うのでしょうか？

以下に、調べて違いを書き出してみましょう。

　　　TOEFLは

　　　結局、TOEICとは

　　　なテストです。

こうしてテキストにもなっているくらいですから、TOEICが大学生にとってポピュラーな英語のテストであることはもう理解出来たでしょう。さて、では大学生の平均点は何点くらいなのでしょうか。これも調べてみてください。

大学生の全国平均点は　　　　　　　点くらい。

では実際の問題を見てみましょう。先のページでリスニング、リーディングがパート別になっていることはわかりましたね。ここでは各パートの例題を示しながら、問題の特徴を大まかに掴みます。各パートの詳しい説明はこれから学ぶ各Unitで詳しく紹介していきますが、まずはどのくらい正解できるのか、例題でチェックしましょう。

Part 1 ● 写真描写問題

以下の写真を説明するのに最もふさわしい英文をひとつ、聞き取って選ぶ問題です。
写真を見ながら問題を解いてみましょう。

♪2

Ⓐ Ⓑ Ⓒ Ⓓ

ここでは (D) She's looking for files in a cabinet. が正解です。

スクリプトを確認してみましょう。

(A) She's seated at a desk.　　(B) She's leaning against a wall.

(C) She's looking out a window.　　(D) She's looking for files in a cabinet.

＊テストでは英文、選択肢は印刷されていません。リスニングなので聞き取って正解をマークします。パート1は全部で6問です。

Unit 1 | What is TOEIC?

Part 2 ● 応答文問題

音声の問いかけ（質問文）に対して正しい応答をひとつ選ぶ問題です。
問題を解いてみましょう。

(3)　　　　　　　　　　　　　　　　　　　　　　　　　　　　Ⓐ Ⓑ Ⓒ

ここでは **(B) Second floor.**（2階です）が正解です。

スクリプトを確認してみましょう。

❶ Where is the meeting room?

(A) On Friday.　(B) Second floor.　(C) I like it.

＊テストでは質問文も応答もどちらも印刷されていません。こうした応答が25問出題されます。

Part 3 ● 会話文問題

会話文を聞いた後、その内容に関する設問に対し、正しい答えを選ぶ問題です。
まずは問題を解いてみましょう。（実際のパート3は3問1セットです。）

(4) **Questions 1 through 2 refer to the following conversation.**

❶ What is the problem?

(A) An incorrect file was sent.　(B) A meeting room was booked.

(C) Some complaints were reported.　(D) A name was misspelled.

Ⓐ Ⓑ Ⓒ Ⓓ

❷ What will the woman do next?

(A) Submit a report　(B) Call a customer

(C) See a client　(D) Collect personal belongings

Ⓐ Ⓑ Ⓒ Ⓓ

1番は **(A) An incorrect file was sent.**（不正確なファイルが送られた）
2番は **(C) See a client**（顧客に会う）が正解です。

スクリプトを確認してみましょう。下線部が解答のヒントです。

M: After this morning's meeting, you said that you would send me a list of the names of the new employees in our department. 1. However, the one you provided me with was from the last year's.

W: I'm very sorry about that. Is it all right to give you the correct one later? 2. I have to go to see an important client immediately, so I don't have enough time right now.

M: That's fine. I'd appreciate if you could send it to me by tomorrow morning.

*テストでは会話のスクリプトは印刷されていません。設問である質問文は一度だけ読み上げられます。ひとつの会話に対して設問が3つずつ用意されており、それが全部で13セット、計39問です。

Part 4 ● トーク問題

（一人のスピーカーが話す）トークを聞いた後、その内容に関する設問に対し、正しい答えを選ぶ問題です。まずは解いてみましょう。

(5)

❶ What is the purpose of the talk?

(A) To describe a service　(B) To learn about a product

(C) To introduce a new employee　(D) To announce a retirement

Ⓐ Ⓑ Ⓒ Ⓓ

❷ What does the speaker ask the listeners to do?

(A) Arrange an appointment　(B) Leave a review of a product

(C) Come up with an idea　(D) Contact the person in charge

Ⓐ Ⓑ Ⓒ Ⓓ

1番は(D) To announce a retirement（退職を知らせるため）、

2番は(C) Come up with an idea（アイデアを出す）が正解です。

スクリプトを確認してみましょう。下線部がヒントです。

Questions 1 through 2 refer to the following talk.

Before we wrap up the meeting, I have an important announcement to make. 1. Ms. Yamada, the director of sales department, has decided to retire next month. This is because she'd like to be closer to her family who live in a different country. So, why don't we celebrate her retirement before she leaves our company? 2. Could you possibly organize your thoughts on a party by the next meeting? I'm looking forward to your excellent ideas.

*テストではトークのスクリプトは印刷されていません。設問の質問は一度だけ読み上げられます。ひとつのトークに対して設問が3つずつ用意されており、それが全部で10セット、計30問です。

Reading ⋯

Part 5 ● 文法、語彙問題

Gray Technology's latest smartphone is affordable compared with ------- items produced by its competitors.

    (A) similarities   (B) similar   (C) similarly   (D) similarity

Ⓐ Ⓑ Ⓒ Ⓓ

ここでは (B) similar（【形容詞】同様の）が正解です。

設問文に設けられた空所に適切な語（句）を４つの選択肢の中からひとつ選ぶ問題です。主に文法、あるいは語彙の知識が問われていて、30問出題されます。

Part 6 ● 文法、語彙、文脈理解問題

例題では１問のみ示していますが、英文のパッセージにこのように４か所の空所が設けられ、それぞれに適切な語（句）、または文、を４つの選択肢の中からひとつ選ぶ問題です。
（今回は例題のため、一つだけ問題をつけています）

To: All staff

We had more success than the year before, and would like to thank all of you for your hard work. As usual, we ------- to hold a special event this evening for all of you. This
1.
year, the party will take place at the main conference room on December 20 at 7:00 P.M. We invite you and your family.

We're offering a special dinner to all attendees. Therefore, please send an email to Glenn of the Human Resources department at gln@umail.com, and let him know whether you are planning to come with your family or not.

Thank you!

    (A) plans   (B) planned   (C) are planning   (D) is planning

Ⓐ Ⓑ Ⓒ Ⓓ

ここでは (C) are planning が正解です。

パート6では、ひとつのパッセージにつき４つの設問があり、それが４セット（４文書）で計16問あります。

Part 7 ● 読解問題

いわゆる読解問題です。メールや記事、チャット画面などを読み、それに関する設問に答える問題です。

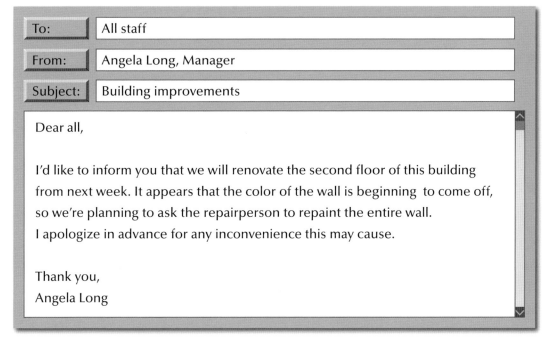

Why was the memo written?

      (A) To make suggestions about remodeling

      (B) To report some complaints

      (C) To ask employees to paint the wall

      (D) To notify employees about a renovation   Ⓐ Ⓑ Ⓒ Ⓓ

ここでは (D) To notify employees about a renovation が正解です。

例題のため、ここでは1つだけ設問がありますが、実際は1つのセットに2問から5問の設問がついています。

その中に、1つの文書を読んで2問から4問の設問に答えるシングルパッセージ (SP)、2つもしくは3つの文書を読んで5問の問題に答えるダブルパッセージ (DP)、トリプルパッセージ (TP) があります。通例、DPは2セット10問、TPは3セット15問で、読解問題の後半に出題されます。

ここまで各パートの形式を確認してきました。

さて、TOEIC L&Rテストは漠然となんとなく勉強しても効果が出にくいテストです。やるからにはしっかり目標を持って学んでいきましょう。よって、各Unitを学習していく前に、何点くらいを目標とするのか、各自の目標を決めましょう。また、これまでに一度でも受けたことのある人はその点数

を書いておき、そこからあと何点スコアをアップさせたいのか決めておきましょう。一度もTOEICを受験したことのない場合は、前半で検索した大学生の平均点である440点程度をスタートラインとして一応決めておきましょう。

TOEICのスコアアップには「学習の時間確保」と「正しいトレーニング」が必要です。
また、1点スコアアップをさせるのに、1時間の学習が必要だと言われています。これを基に、スコアアップするのに必要な学習時間を確保しましょう。

■ 受けたことのある人

　　　前回の得点（総点）　　　　　点

　　　（受けたことのない人は、大学生の平均点である440点程度を目安に書いておきましょう）

　　　リスニング　　　　　点　　　　リーディング　　　　　点

■ これから取ってみたい目標点数

　　　総点　　　　　点

　　　リスニング　　　　　点　　　　リーディング　　　　　点

目標を達成出来るように、今度いつTOEIC L&Rテストを受けるか、決めておきましょう。

　　　私は　　　年　　　月にTOEIC L&Rテストを受験します！

さて、ここからは逆算です。

　　● 目標点を達成するために必要な学習時間は（1点1時間換算で）（　　　　　　　　　）時間。

　　● 目標点を達成するまでに（　　　　　　　　）ヶ月。

　　→ 目標点を達成するには1ヶ月に（　　　　　　　　）時間の学習が必要。

　　→ 目標点を達成するには1週間に（　　　　　　　　）時間の学習が必要。

　　　　　　　　1日（　　　　　　　　）時間はTOEICの学習時間を確保する

また、TOEIC L&Rテストは当然英語のテストですので、これまでの英語の知識をうまく活かしましょう。英語が苦手、という人もせっかくのこの機会に英語が好きになれるよう、勉強法などを考えてみましょう。では以下の質問に対するみなさんなりの答えを書き出してみてください。

■ これまでやった英語学習の中で効果があったのはどんな学習法でしたか？

■ これまでやった英語学習の中であまり効果がなかったのはどんな学習法でしたか？

ペアで、グループで、比べてみましょう。人それぞれですから、正解などはもちろんありません。自分にあった学習法を見つけましょう。

もし、ペアで、グループで話した中で自分も試してみたい、という学習法があったらメモしておきましょう。

■ メモ

このテキストはTOEIC L&Rテストを扱いますが、英語、特に文法事項など、の全ての学習項目（高校までの既習事項）を説明して網羅出来るわけではありません。必要に応じて、これまで高校の時に使った参考書などを参照してください。以下に、自分が持っている英語の参考書（TOEIC L&Rテスト対策のものがあればそれも）を書き出してみましょう。どれがこれからの学習に使えそうでしょうか。

ではまとめです。

目標を今一度整理しましょう。

私は（　　　）年（　　　）月に受験し（　　　）点（リスニング（　　　）点、リーディング（　　　）点）を目指します。そのために、（　　　　　　　　　　　　　　　　）という勉強法をやってみます。また、学習時間を1週間に（　　　　　　　）時間確保します。

書いたら、ペアで、グループで上記をお互い宣言しましょう。

さあ、ではこれからTOEICの学習をこのテキストを使って始めていきましょう。

↪ *Review for Today's Lesson*

What did you learn today?

では今日学んだことを自分の言葉でまとめておきましょう。
まとめられたらペアの人とお互いに確認してください。

■ 来週までにするべき課題、自分の目標

自分の目標をしっかりペアの人に宣言し、終わりましょう。

Unit 2

本日の学習項目

Part 2 | Part 5

 Listening ‥‥

Part 2 説明　パート2は短い質問文に対する正しい応答を選ぶ問題です。Unit 1で確認したように、選択肢は3つで、質問、応答、共にテスト用紙には印刷されていません。ではまずどのようなタイプの質問文があるのか、確認してみましょう。

● WH疑問文

WHで始まる疑問詞、when, where, what, who, why, how などで始まる疑問文です。このパターンの場合、最初の疑問詞が聞き取れるかどうかで正解できる／できないが決まってしまう場合が多いです。集中して文頭を聞くように心がけてください。

● Yes/No 疑問文

答えが yes か no で答えられる、普通の疑問文パターンです。しかし、yes／no と言ったとしてもそれだけでは正解にはなりません。関係ないことを答えている選択肢は間違いですので、最後まで応答文を聞きましょう。

● 平叙文

いわゆる普通の文です。誰かの一言にフォローを入れるようなイメージです。日本語で、普段の日常的な会話を思い浮かべてみるとわかりやすいでしょう。

● 付加疑問文

平叙文の後に isn't it? や don't you? のような表現が続き、「〜ですよね？」という意味が付加される疑問文です。頻度はあまり多くはありませんが、出題される疑問文のうちのひとつです。

● 選択・否定疑問文

Which を用いて A か B のどちらかを尋ねる、選択式の疑問文です。A か B のどちらかを選ぶものが正解になるのが普通ですが、そうではない若干ひっかけ的な意地悪な答え方があったりもします。また、文頭が Don't you 〜？などで始まるも疑問文は否定疑問文と呼ばれ、「〜しないの？」と問いかけています。

パート2では似たような音を含む応答文（選択肢）をわざと用いる、音ワナというひっかけがあります。これは大抵、間違いの選択肢として用意されています。coffee／copy machineのように、なんとなく聞いていると同じ音に聞こえてしまう場合があり、それを根拠に「正解だ！」としないようにしましょう。

Part 2 ● 応答文問題

では実際の問題をまず一度やってみましょう。

質問文のあとに３つの応答文が読まれます。一番適切なものを選びましょう。

(6)　❶ Mark your answer.　　　(A) (B) (C)

(7)　❷ Mark your answer.　　　(A) (B) (C)

(8)　❸ Mark your answer.　　　(A) (B) (C)

(9)　❹ Mark your answer.　　　(A) (B) (C)

(10)　❺ Mark your answer.　　　(A) (B) (C)

(11)　❻ Mark your answer.　　　(A) (B) (C)

(12)　❼ Mark your answer.　　　(A) (B) (C)

(13)　❽ Mark your answer.　　　(A) (B) (C)

(14)　❾ Mark your answer.　　　(A) (B) (C)

(15)　❿ Mark your answer.　　　(A) (B) (C)

Exercise Questions! 🚶

今聞いた音声の大切な部分（文頭やキーワード）だけを聞き取り、書き取ってみましょう。

❶　　　　　❷　　　　　❸　　　　　❹

❺　　　　　❻　　　　　❼　　　　　❽

❾　　　　　❿

More Exercise Questions! 🚶🚶

ペアで、グループで比べてみましょう。どんな単語を書き取りましたか？また、なぜそれが大切だと思いましたか？

先ほどの問題を、今度は音声を聞きながら穴埋めしてみましょう。

(6)　❶　(　　　　　) did you find this (　　　　　)?

　　　(A) Friday evening.　　(B) On your desk.　　(C) I haven't found it yet.

　　　　　　　　　　　　　　　　　　　　　　　　　(A) (B) (C)

(7)　❷　(　　　　　) will write the (　　　　　) for the next meeting?

　　　(A) John will do.　　(B) The meeting was over.　　(C) I remember the writer.

　　　　　　　　　　　　　　　　　　　　　　　　　(A) (B) (C)

(8) ❸ Can you pick me up in front of the (   ) (   ) later?

(A) Yes, I will post it.   (B) Sorry, I'm not available.

(C) This is the official letter.   Ⓐ Ⓑ Ⓒ

(9) ❹ Do I need to (   ) my identification card?

(A) Yes, please.   (B) It was a nice show.

(C) No, you can't park your car here.   Ⓐ Ⓑ Ⓒ

(10) ❺ I think this semester will be (   ).

(A) Our business has been successful.   (B) We have already had many assignments.

(C) This is yours, not mine.   Ⓐ Ⓑ Ⓒ

(11) ❻ I forgot my password for my (   ).

(A) Commuter train has arrived.   (B) Where will you get it?

(C) Why don't you ask the security office?   Ⓐ Ⓑ Ⓒ

(12) ❼ This (   ) is so delicious, isn't it?

(A) Chocolate, please.   (B) There was a piece on it in a magazine last week.

(C) Kate is here.   Ⓐ Ⓑ Ⓒ

(13) ❽ Mike should be invited to the (   ), shouldn't he?

(A) He has his confidence about the machine.   (B) I agree.

(C) Sunday is the best.   Ⓐ Ⓑ Ⓒ

(14) ❾ Which one should we go to, (   ) or bus stop?

(A) The train has been delayed.   (B) The stationary is ready.

(C) Stop writing.   Ⓐ Ⓑ Ⓒ

(15) ❿ Aren't you (   ) to the movie theater tonight?

(A) Yes, I like hamburgers.   (B) No, Sandy is going instead.

(C) There are many pens to write with.   Ⓐ Ⓑ Ⓒ

Exercise Questions! 🚶🚶 ≫≫≫

正しい応答に○をつけましょう。また、音ワナが使われている箇所に線を引いてみましょう。終わったら、ペアで、グループでくらべてみましょう。

More Exercise Questions! 🚶🚶 ≫≫≫

次に、質問文と正しい応答文を用いて、一問一答形式でお互いに会話してみましょう。
出来るようになったら、今度は応答文を見ないでアドリブで設問文に答えてみましょう。

Reading ....

Part 5 説明

Unit 1で見たように、Part 5は空所に語（句）を入れる問題でしたね。

この問題は大きく分けて、文法と語彙、の2種類に分かれます。文法はその名の通り文法事項に関する問いなので、知っていれば瞬時に解答出来ますが、逆に知らないとその日その場で解答するのは（ほぼ）不可能でしょう。語彙は単語の意味が問われているので、こちらも知らなければ基本的にアウトです。言い換えると、このパートは知識が問われているので、わからなかった際に無駄に時間を費やさないことがポイントです。ですので、目安としては1問最大で20秒、それ以上考えても知らない、わからないと判断したら即座にどれかを（適当に）マークしてその日はそれ以上無駄に勝負しないことをおススメします。

よって、1問20秒だと3問1分、30問出題されるので（　　）分でこのパートを駆け抜けるのが理想です。

ただし、設問によっては空所の近くだけを読めば解ける問題もあります。

1. 最初に選択肢をチェック

2. 空所の近くだけを読めば解ける問題かどうかをチェック

    (1) 空所の近くだけを読めば解けそうなら5秒を目安に解く

    (2) 空所の近く以外も読んで解く問題は、20秒以内を目安に解く

3. 知らない問題は捨てる

これを心がけ、トータルで10分以内を目指しましょう。

主に問われる文法事項としては、

  品詞（名詞、動詞、形容詞、副詞、単数と複数などの見分け、使い分け）

    例 ▶ success / succeed / successful / successfully // store / stores

  動詞の形（時制や態、現在/過去分詞など）

    例 ▶ make / makes / made / making / have made / have been making

  代名詞（格を問う問題）

    例 ▶ he / his / him / himself

  関係代名詞

    例 ▶ that / what / which / whose / whom など

  前置詞

    例 ▶ in / on / at / of / with / under など

  接続詞

    例 ▶ and / though / however / so that などがあります。

語彙の場合は同じ品詞（名詞、動詞、形容詞、副詞）のものが選択肢に4つ並びます。その中から設問文に入れて意味が通るものを選びます。以下のように、同じ品詞で意味の違う単語が4つ並ぶケースです。

  名　詞：**例** ▶ production / function / determination / station

  動　詞：**例** ▶ consist / inspect / expect / expose

  形容詞：**例** ▶ aggresive / persuasive / progressive / permissive

  副　詞：**例** ▶ accidentally / meaningfully / progressively / certainly

ただし、「前置詞vs接続詞」と呼ばれるタイプの問題は、語彙問題ですが文法の知識を使って解きます。例えば as long as（接続詞）/ along with（前置詞）/ however（副詞）/ otherwise（副詞）のような問題です。

この場合は、SVの前には接続詞、名詞の前には前置詞を置きます。

Part 5 ● 文法、語彙問題

では実際のPart 5形式の問題をやってみましょう。4つの選択肢の中から一番適切だと思うものを選んでください。

❶ Gregory's Gift Shop will be open ------- Sunday starting in June.

 (A) enough (B) most (C) every (D) little   Ⓐ Ⓑ Ⓒ Ⓓ

❷ Wright Anderson's bags are designed ------- for long-distance travel.

 (A) immediately (B) specifically (C) promptly (D) controversially

                 Ⓐ Ⓑ Ⓒ Ⓓ

❸ Many citizens have expressed ------- to the plan of a new tax system.

 (A) opposition (B) opposing (C) oppose (D) opposes   Ⓐ Ⓑ Ⓒ Ⓓ

❹ After days of heavy rain, the temperature in this town ------- fell slightly last night.

 (A) final (B) finally (C) finalist (D) finals   Ⓐ Ⓑ Ⓒ Ⓓ

❺ To avoid confusion, ------- your name on the tag provided.

 (A) write (B) wrote (C) written (D) writing   Ⓐ Ⓑ Ⓒ Ⓓ

❻ In ------- of the fine seasonal weather, Bella's Italian Café will be opening its patio area for dining.

 (A) considering (B) consideration (C) consider (D) considerable   Ⓐ Ⓑ Ⓒ Ⓓ

❼ Daily expenses that exceed Ryan Design's expense guidelines are not eligible for reimbursement ------- authorization is obtained from a manager.

 (A) however (B) without (C) unless (D) only   Ⓐ Ⓑ Ⓒ Ⓓ

❽ Walsh Auto has issued a report to address concerns ------- the fuel efficiency of its vehicles.

 (A) leading (B) excluding (C) following (D) regarding   Ⓐ Ⓑ Ⓒ Ⓓ

❾ Mr. Landry's promotion means that ------- will supervise a larger team.

 (A) he (B) his (C) him (D) himself   Ⓐ Ⓑ Ⓒ Ⓓ

❿ Employees should remember to shut down ------- computers when leaving for the day.

 (A) their (B) that (C) who (D) its   Ⓐ Ⓑ Ⓒ Ⓓ

Exercise Questions! 🚶🚶 ﹥﹥﹥

今やった問題を分析してみましょう。（　　　）に文法と語彙のどちらが問われているのか、書いてみましょう。また、その選択肢を選んだ理由も書き出してみましょう。書き終わったら、ペアで、グループで、同じかどうか確認してみましょう。

❶　（　　　　　）　**理由** ▶

❷　（　　　　　）　**理由** ▶

❸　（　　　　　）　**理由** ▶

❹　（　　　　　）　**理由** ▶

❺　（　　　　　）　**理由** ▶

❻　（　　　　　）　**理由** ▶

❼　（　　　　　）　**理由** ▶

❽　（　　　　　）　**理由** ▶

❾　（　　　　　）　**理由** ▶

❿　（　　　　　）　**理由** ▶

More Exercise Questions! 🚶 ﹥﹥﹥

左ページの用紙を用いて、設問文を詳しく分析してみましょう。知らない単語は辞書などで調べて意味を書き込んだり、意味のかたまりごとにスラッシュを入れたりして、一文を正確に理解しましょう。

↷*Review for Today's Lesson*

What did you learn today?

では今日学んだことを自分の言葉でまとめておきましょう。
まとめられたらペアの人とお互いに確認してください。

■ リスニングについて

■ リーディングについて

■ 来週までにするべき課題、自分の目標

自分の目標をしっかりペアの人に宣言し、終わりましょう。

Unit 3

本日の学習項目

Part 1 | Part 7 SP (Single Passage)-1

 Listening ‥‥

Part 1 説明	パート１は、問題冊子に印刷された写真の説明として一番ふさわしいものを選ぶ問題で、選択肢が４つ音声として流れます（英文は印刷されていません）。写真には大きく分けて４つのパターンがあります。

❶ 人物１人が写真の中心に写っているもの

→ 人物の動作、何をしているか、服装、持ち物などに注意します。

❷ 人物２人ないし３人以上が写真の中心に写っているもの

→ 人物それぞれの動作、何をしているか、２人または３人の関係性、服装、持ち物などに注意します。

❸ 人以外のモノが写真の中心に写っているもの　＊人物は写っていません。

→ モノがどういう状態にあるのか、に注意します。

❹ モノと人物が一緒に写っているもの

→ 人物が何をしているのか、どんなモノが写っているのか、に注意します。

上記４パターンのいずれであっても、写っていないものが正解になることはありません。必ず写っているものに関する英文があるはずですので、それを聞き逃さないようにしましょう。やり方としては以下を参考にしてください。

　　　❶ 写真を見て上記のどのパターンか見分ける。
　　　❷ 写真にどんなものが写っているのか、どんな単語が頭に浮かぶか、を確認する。
　　　❸ 音声をしっかり聞いてマークする。

なお、聞いている間に混乱しないよう、少しでも「そうかな？」と思った選択肢には軽く印をつけておくか、指で押さえておくと忘れないでおけるので効果的です。

Exercise Questions! 🚶

以下の単語はパート１に頻出と言われている単語です。いくつ意味を知っていますか？

[utensil / wheelbarrow / appliance / vehicle / vessel / lean against]

More Exercise Questions! 🚶

以下の文章はパート１に頻出と言われている表現を用いた例文です。例文の意味がわかりますか？

The buildings are reflected on the water.

Electric appliances are unplugged.

Part 1 ● 写真描写問題

4つの音声の中から写真の説明として一番適切なものを選びましょう。

(16) ❶  メモ

Ⓐ Ⓑ Ⓒ Ⓓ

(17) ❷  メモ

Ⓐ Ⓑ Ⓒ Ⓓ

(18) ❸  メモ

Ⓐ Ⓑ Ⓒ Ⓓ

(19) ❹  メモ

Ⓐ Ⓑ Ⓒ Ⓓ

Exercise Questions! 🚶 ▸▸▸

前のページの問題のスクリプトです。正解の根拠を確認しましょう。写真の説明として重要な語句に線を引いてみましょう。また、それぞれの選択肢を音読してみましょう。

(16) ❶ (A) She is looking at the mirror.
(B) She is relaxing on the bench.
(C) She is standing on the floor.
(D) She is talking on the phone.

(A) 彼女は鏡を見ているところだ。　(B) 彼女はベンチでリラックスしているところだ。
(C) 彼女は床の上に立っているところだ。　(D) 彼女は電話で話しているところだ。

(17) ❷ (A) A woman is collecting stamps.
(B) A man and a woman are walking side by side.
(C) A man is bringing some documents.
(D) A man and a woman are talking outside of a building.

(A) 女性は切手を集めているところだ。　(B) 男性と女性は隣り合って歩いているところだ。
(C) 男性は複数の書類を持ってきているところだ。　(D) 男性と女性は建物の外で話しているところだ。

(18) ❸ (A) There are trees along the river.
(b) The lamp is situated inside the garden.
(c) Cars are parked in front of houses.
(d) The road is occupied by buses.

(A) 川に沿って複数の木がある。　(B) ランプが庭の中にある。
(C) 複数の車が家の前に駐車されている。　(D) 道は複数のバスで占拠されている。

(19) ❹ (A) They are looking at a map.
(B) They are wearing T-shirts.
(C) They are preparing a meal.
(D) They are showing identification cards.

(A) 彼らは地図を見ているところだ。　(B) 彼らはTシャツを着ている。
(C) 彼らは食事を準備しているところだ。　(D) 彼らは身分証明書を見せているところだ。

More Exercise Questions! 🚶🚶 ▸▸▸

前ページのメモ欄に、写真に写っているものを英語で書き出してみましょう。終わったらペアでくらべましょう。

Reading ⋯

<table>
<tr><td>

**Part 7
シングル
パッセージ
の特徴**

</td><td>

このUnitではパート7の中でも、シングルパッセージと呼ばれる、文書が1つだけの読解問題のパターンを学習します。文書はメール、広告、記事など様々なものがあります。いずれにしても、基本的に文書はすべて読むようにしてください。飛ばし読みなど、一部分しか読まないで問題を解こうとすると、かえって情報をうまく掴めず、結果として余計に時間がかかってしまいます。

</td></tr>
</table>

設問の特徴としては、以下のような設問であることが多いので、どのパターンの設問があるのかを見極めて取り組むとよいでしょう。

文書全体の主題、テーマを問う全体問題

例 ▶ What is the purpose of the e-mail? /
What is the main topic of the article?

文書の一部の詳細を問う個別問題

例 ▶ How can guests obtain a free item? /
In what department does Mr. Lee most likely work?

文書には書いていないことを問うNOT問題

例 ▶ What is NOT mentioned as a reason for the sales increase? /
What did Mr. Santos NOT do during the last year?

なお、解く時間の目安は1問1分です。パート7は全部で54問 (Questions147-200) あるので、このペースでやって54分かかります。公開テストの終了時刻から逆算するとパート7に55分確保するとちょうど終わる計算となります。

そもそも、パート7に55分の時間を残すには、パート5 (30問) を10分、パート6 (16問) を10分で解く必要があります。この時間配分は必ず覚えておきましょう。リーディングは試験時間の管理 (タイムマネジメント) がとても大切です。

ただし、600-700点を目指す人は、200番まで全て解く必要はありません。最後まできちんと読んで解く必要があるのは上級者だけです。例えば600点を取るのに必要なリーディグセクション300点を取る場合、最後まで解き終わらずに塗り絵 (業界用語で適当に塗ること) をしても良いのです。15問ほど塗り絵をしても、解いた問題を確実に正解できるようにしていけば、300点は取れます。

Part 7 ● 読解問題

ではPart 7の問題を実際にやってみましょう。制限時間は設問の数に合わせてそれぞれ2分、3分、3分です。

Questions 1-2 refer to the following e-mail.

To:	\<questions@parkplacehotel.com\>
From:	dereksimmons@aboutmail.com
Subject:	Inquiry
Date:	July 16

Dear Sir or Madam,

I am writing to ask for the availability of a banquet room on August 30. My collegue recently won a prestigious award by the Texas Construction Society, and I plan to celebrate this occasion. I am looking for a room that can accommodate about 100 guests. The party will take place on August 30. Do you have any rooms that are available on that day?

Best regards,
Derek Simmons

❶ What is the purpose of the e-mail?

(A) To advertise a property   (B) To announce a new policy

(C) To find a place for a party   (D) To apply for a job

Ⓐ Ⓑ Ⓒ Ⓓ

❷ When will the party be held?

(A) July 15   (B) July 16

(C) August 29   (D) August 30

Ⓐ Ⓑ Ⓒ Ⓓ

Questions 3-5 refer to the following announcement.

■ To All Employees

Results from our customer satisfaction survey, which was conducted at some of the electronic retail stores across our county, showed a high level of satisfaction with our new smartphone. The survey was released on April 10, and continued to be taken until July 10. Nearly 90% of those surveyed commented that they were satisfied with its durability, picture quality, and user-friendliness. On the other hand, more than 70% said that the price wasn't affordable. This was the worst part of the rating in the survey.

❸ What is the announcement mainly about?

(A) Sales figures   (B) Customer satisfaction survey

(C) Product specifications   (D) Market trend

Ⓐ Ⓑ Ⓒ Ⓓ

❹ What is NOT mentioned as a feature of the product?

(A) Durability   (B) Picture quality

(C) User-friendliness   (D) Battery life

Ⓐ Ⓑ Ⓒ Ⓓ

❺ For how long was the survey conducted?

(A) Three weeks   (B) A month

(C) Two months   (D) Three months

Ⓐ Ⓑ Ⓒ Ⓓ

Questions 6-8 refer to the following advertisement.

Gadget Solutions

Are you looking for some equipment for an event? Look no further than Gadget Solutions. We guarantee that your event will be successful, due largely in part to the equipment we can rent you.

EQUIPMENT you can use

- Monitor ● Projector
- Wireless microphone
- Large screen ● Sound system

Please feel free to talk to any one of the Gadget Solutions employees, should you have any questions regarding the items. They have the expertise to help you find and select the appropriate equipment for your event.

❻ What is being advertised?

(A) A discount sale　(B) An annual program

(C) A promotional event　(D) Rental services

Ⓐ Ⓑ Ⓒ Ⓓ

❼ What item is NOT listed in the advertisement?

(A) Monitor　(B) Laptop computer

(C) Projector　(D) Microphone

Ⓐ Ⓑ Ⓒ Ⓓ

❽ What do Gadget Solutions employees do for customers?

(A) Repair digital devices　(B) Arrange an event

(C) Help choose equipment　(D) Deliver an item

Ⓐ Ⓑ Ⓒ Ⓓ

Exercise Questions! 🚶 ＞＞＞

前ページでやったパート７の問題を分析してみましょう。どういうタイプ（全体、個別、NOT）の問題だったでしょうか？

❶（　　　　）❷（　　　　）

❸（　　　）❹（　　　）❺（　　　　）

❻（　　　）❼（　　　）❽（　　　　）

More *Exercise Questions!* 🚶🚶 ＞＞＞

問題文の用紙を使って、今度はもう少し正確に読んでみましょう。ここでは線を引いたり、単語に丸をつけたりしてもかまいません。正解の根拠となる部分をしっかりつかみましょう。終わったら、ペアで、グループで、それらを確認してみましょう。なお、時間は先生の指示に従ってください。

↘ *Review for Today's Lesson*

What did you learn today?

では今日学んだことを自分の言葉でまとめておきましょう。
まとめられたらペアの人と意見交換してください。

■ リスニングについて

■ リーディングについて

■ 来週までにするべき課題、自分の目標

自分の目標をしっかりペアの人に宣言し終わりましょう。

Part 3-1 | Part 6

 **Listening** …

Part 3 説明	Part 3は会話文を聞いて答える問題です。Unit 1で確認したように、各会話文に（　　）つの設問があり、全部で（　　）セット、計（　　）問のセクションです。リスニングなので当然、会話が聞き取れないといけないのですが、それと同じくらい問題を解く際に重要なことがあります。それは設問文や選択肢を、会話を聞く前に読んでおく「先読み」と呼ばれるテクニックです。例えば、天気予報を日本語で聞いていたとしましょう。何も注意を払わずぼーっと聞いた後で、突然「○○県の明日の夜の天気は？」と聞かれて、即座に答えられるでしょうか？たぶん、無理です。しかし、「○○県の明日の夜の天気だけは聞いておかないと」と心の中で強く決めていたらどうでしょうか？そこに最大限注意して聞きますよね？つまり、先読みとは知りたい情報、知らないといけない情報とは何か、を把握することなのです。よって、問題先読み → リスニング → 解答する、のリズムを体内に感覚として作っておくことが肝心です。

なお、Part 3ではよく出る会話の場面、ポイントがありますのでそれらをあらかじめ知っておくことも大切な準備です。以下にまとめておきますので、どういう会話がなされそうか、想像してみてください。

> **オフィス / 受付もしくは医者 / ショップ / レストラン / 駅や空港**

このUnitでは会話の基本形、A → B → A → Bのやりとり（2往復といいます）を用いて練習します。典型的な会話の流れとしては以下のようになります。

> A すみません、エアコンの調子が悪いのですが。
>
> B 電源を入れ直してみましたか？
>
> A ええ、それでも動かないんです。
>
> B では業者に連絡してみますね。

簡単にいうと、トラブル発生 → 反応する → それに対しリアクション → 解決策、のような感じで、問題解決型の会話であることが多いです。

また、設問も2パターンがあり、会話全体のテーマやトピックを尋ねる「全体」問題と、1か所にしか出てこない詳細を尋ねる「個別」問題があります。よって、問題がどんな情報を聞き取る問題なのかを意識しておくとよいでしょう。

> 「全体」問題の設問文例：What is the purpose of this talk?
>
> 「個別」問題の設問文例：When will the conference be held?

Part 3 ● 会話文問題

では会話を聞いて正しい答えをひとつ、選んでみましょう。

⟨20⟩ **Questions 1 through 3 refer to the following conversation.**

❶ Where most likely is the conversation most likely taking place?

    (A) At a furniture store   (B) At a hardware store

    (C) At a clothing store   (D) At a jewelry store   Ⓐ Ⓑ Ⓒ Ⓓ

❷ What problem does the man mention?

    (A) The item is expensive.   (B) The item is too small.

    (C) The item is damaged.   (D) The item is the wrong design.   Ⓐ Ⓑ Ⓒ Ⓓ

❸ What does the woman suggest the man do?

    (A) Come back tomorrow   (B) Try another store

    (C) Apply for a refund   (D) Consider another item   Ⓐ Ⓑ Ⓒ Ⓓ

(21) Questions 4 through 6 refer to the following conversation.

❹ What are the speakers mainly discussing?

    (A) A budget proposal   (B) A news report

    (C) Some test results   (D) Some new clients   Ⓐ Ⓑ Ⓒ Ⓓ

❺ What will happen in August?

    (A) A new branch will be open.   (B) A new security system will be installed.

    (C) Employees will attend an event.   (D) Clients will visit the office.

    Ⓐ Ⓑ Ⓒ Ⓓ

❻ What will the woman do next?

    (A) Make a phone call   (B) Contact a colleague

    (C) Send an e-mail   (D) Inform her supervisor   Ⓐ Ⓑ Ⓒ Ⓓ

(22) Question 7 through 9 refer to the following conversation.

❼ Where does the conversation most likely take place?

    (A) At a hotel   (B) At a restaurant

    (C) At a travel agency   (D) At a supermarket   Ⓐ Ⓑ Ⓒ Ⓓ

❽ What does the man say he must do?

    (A) Revise a schedule   (B) Meet with a client

    (C) Attend a meeting   (D) Pay by cash   Ⓐ Ⓑ Ⓒ Ⓓ

❾ What does the woman suggest the man do?

    (A) Order some drinks   (B) Participate in a drawing

    (C) Check a web site   (D) Fill out a form   Ⓐ Ⓑ Ⓒ Ⓓ

Exercise Questions! 🚶🚶 ⟫⟫⟫

以下は先の問題のスクリプトです。音声を聞いて空所に入る単語を書き取ってみましょう。また、先の問題が「全体」問題か「個別」問題か識別してみましょう。出来たら、ペアで、グループで、同じかどうか確認してみましょう。

(20) Questions 1 through 3 refer to the following conversation.

M: I want to (   ) these trousers. I tried them on, but I think I'll need a (   ) size. All of the labels are still attached.

W: Okay, that shouldn't be a problem. I just need to see your receipt.

M: Wait a moment. Ah... here it is. I was also wondering if I could change the (   ) to gray instead of navy.

W: I'm very sorry, but we've sold out of the gray. You are welcome to look at some other (   ), if you like.

❶ (   ) ❷ (   ) ❸ (   )

(21) Questions 4 through 6 refer to the following conversation.

M: Hi, Laura. Welcome back from your trip. Did you manage to find any new clients?

W: Well, yes and no. There was a lot of (   ) in Seoul with four new companies deciding to stock our products. Despite high expectations, I only (   ) to secure one new client in Tokyo.

M: Five new (   ) are still a very good effort. These will definitely help the company stay on track to achieve its sales forecasts. Besides, marketing will be (   ) a team to Japan in August for the International Fashion Expo. I'm sure they'll secure some more clients.

W: Let's hope so. Anyway, I'd better get these signed contracts off to Georgina in accounts.

❹ (   ) ❺ (   ) ❻ (   )

(22) Questions 7 through 9 refer to the following conversation.

W: How did you like your meal? I hope you like the pasta. Do you want to try one of our desserts?

M: The pasta was marvelous. Desserts sound great, but actually, I'm in a bit of a (   ). I have a staff meeting that I need to attend. Could I have a (   ), please? I'll pay by my credit card.

W: Certainly. Oh, just one thing. It won't take long. To (   ) our 5-year anniversary, we have a (   ) meal ticket competition. If you put your business card in this box, we randomly draw a card and (   ) the winner.

M: That sounds great. Here's my business card.

❼ (   ) ❽ (   ) ❾ (   )

More Exercise Questions! 🚶

答え合わせが終わったらリスニング力をあげるためにも音読の練習をたくさんしましょう。何度も練習して、スピード、発音、共に問題の音声に近づけることが出来るよう練習しましょう。

More & *More* Exercise Questions! 🚶🚶

ペアで会話してみましょう。出来るようになったら、どちらかがスクリプトを見ずにアドリブで答えてみましょう。どんな会話になるでしょうか？

📖 Reading ····

Part 6
説明 Part 6は文書を読み、空所に適切な語（句）または文を入れる問題です。1文書に対して4問、4文書あるので合計16問の設問があります。時間配分としては1問30秒、つまり1文書に約2分、Part 6全体で約8分が理想の解答時間です。先に学習したPart 5が約10分でしたので、おおまかに言うとPart 5, 6で合計約20分、これらのパートを公開テストでリスニング終了後すぐにやるとすると約20分後にこの2パートを終えられるのが理想です。もちろん、解答する順序は必ずしも前から順番通りに、でなくてもよいので、Part 5から7を5→7→6、や6→7→5、7→6→5などのようにやってもかまいません。いずれであってもPart 5, 6で合計約20分、Part 6全体で約8分、が守られればどの順序であってもよいです。

さて、Part 6には2つのタイプの設問、独立型と文脈型、が存在します。独立型とは、文書の流れを必ずしも理解する必要はなく、該当する一文のみをしっかり見れば解ける問題、いわば形を変えたPart（　　　）です。文法を問われることが多いので、先にやった文法、語彙の見極めがここで生きてきます。文脈型はその逆で、文書の流れがわかっていないと答えられない問題です。この場合は少なくとも前後の2、3文の流れが掴めないと手がかりを得ることが出来ません。その究極の形が文挿入問題で、一文まるごと正しい文を入れないといけないので、初級者には手ごわい問題でしょう。なお、この文挿入問題はその該当箇所が文頭、文中、文尾のどこであれ、他の問題を解き終わった最後にやることをおススメします。

■ タイムマネジメントのまとめ（Part 5→6→7の順で試験開始が13時の場合）

13:00　リスニング

13:45　Part 5（30題）＋Part 6（16題）

14:05　Part 7（54題）

15:00　試験終了

Part 6 ● 文法、語彙、文脈理解問題

ではPart 6の問題を実際にやってみましょう。

> Questions 1-4 refer to the following e-mail.

To:	georgeomalley@nnsmail.com
From:	ninar@parkpubishing.com
Subject:	Marketing Strategies Subscription
Date:	October 29

Dear Mr. O'Malley

Thanks for using ------. service for the past year – we love having you as our loyal
customer. ------. We are hoping that it was just a lapse in memory, but we hope that you
would renew your subscription.
1.   **2.**

If you want to continue taking advantage of our magazine and retain all your data and
------., you can easily renew by going to {this page}.
3.

We can also call you sometime next week, so I can show you our new magazines and
answer ------. questions you have. Feel free to book a time using {this link}.
4.

Thank you,

Nina Richards
Customer Service Representative

❶ (A) his   (B) her   (C) our   (D) their   Ⓐ Ⓑ Ⓒ Ⓓ

❷ (A) As a reminder, the warranty you purchased on this product will almost expire.

(B) We will send you a contract with payment and copyright details.

(C) Your subscription of Marketing Strategies will expire in 30days.

(D) For more information, visit our magazine's Web site at www.marketingstrategies.com.

Ⓐ Ⓑ Ⓒ Ⓓ

❸ (A) preferences   (B) preferably   (C) preferable   (D) prefer   Ⓐ Ⓑ Ⓒ Ⓓ

❹ (A) every   (B) each   (C) any   (D) much   Ⓐ Ⓑ Ⓒ Ⓓ

Questions 5-8 refer to the following letter.

Dear Sir or Madam:

My name is Caleb Johnson and I run Central Furnishings, a small furniture design studio
in Northern California. ------, I ------. the Furniture Design and Production Conference
(FDPC) in Texas. ------. They mentioned using your product for cleaning their production
equipment. If possible, I was wondering if I could get a sample of Industrial Super
Detergent to try at my studio. If I think it is useful, I anticipate that I would need roughly 50
liters a year for my main studio as well as an ------. 30 liters per years for my new downtown
studio. Thank you for your help. I look forward to hearing from you.
5.   **6.**   **7.**   **8.**

Caleb Johnson
Luminescent Designs

❺ (A) Probably　(B) Alternatively　(C) Totally　(D) Recently　　Ⓐ Ⓑ Ⓒ Ⓓ

❻ (A) was attended　(B) attended　(C) will attend　(D) will be attended　Ⓐ Ⓑ Ⓒ Ⓓ

❼ (A) While I was there, I talked to several other studio owners.

　　(B) Therefore, I planned to attend a job fair.

　　(C) The new furniture is schedule to be delivered on May 30.

　　(D) However, I have attended FDPC in the past.　　Ⓐ Ⓑ Ⓒ Ⓓ

❽ (A) additionally　(B) additional　(C) add　(D) addition　　Ⓐ Ⓑ Ⓒ Ⓓ

Exercise Questions! 🚶🚶 ▸▸▸

ここでは今やった問題を分析してみましょう。（　　　）に独立型と文脈型のいずれであるのか、書いてみましょう。また、その選択肢を選んだ理由も書き出してみましょう。書き終わったら、ペアで、グループで、同じかどうか確認してみましょう。

❶（　　　）理由 ▸　　　　　　　❺（　　　）理由 ▸

❷（　　　）理由 ▸　　　　　　　❻（　　　）理由 ▸

❸（　　　）理由 ▸　　　　　　　❼（　　　）理由 ▸

❹（　　　）理由 ▸　　　　　　　❽（　　　）理由 ▸

More Exercise Questions! 🚶 ▸▸▸

左ページの用紙を用いて、設問文を詳しく分析してみましょう。知らない単語は辞書などで調べて意味を書き込んだり、意味のかたまりごとにスラッシュを入れたりして、一文を正確に理解しましょう。

↷ *Review for Today's Lesson*

What did you learn today?

では今日学んだことを自分の言葉でまとめておきましょう。
まとめられたらペアの人と確認してください。

■ リスニングについて

■ リーディングについて

■ 来週までにするべき課題、自分の目標

自分の目標をしっかりペアの人に宣言し、終わりましょう。

本日の学習項目

Part 3-2 | Part 7 SP (Single Passage) -2

Part 3 -2-

Unit 4ではPart 3の基本的なパターン、パートの概要を学びました。このUnitでは Part 3の中でも若干難易度が高い、あるいは一見複雑そうな問題を扱います。Part 3 の基本形、A → B → A → Bの2往復以外のパターンとして以下のものがあります。

長めの会話 ／ 3人の会話 ／ グラフィック ／

意図問題 (*この問題については Part 4、Part 7のところで改めて解説します。)

長めの会話とは、A → B → A → Bのあとにさらに会話が続き、結果として3往復以上になっている ものを指します。この場合はやりとりが長くなっただけで、設問で問われる内容は2往復のものと何 ら変わりはありません。

3人の会話とは、A、BだけでなくCも登場し、3人で話が進行する状況です。大抵、男性2人と女 性1人、あるいは女性2人と男性1人、からなっていて、全員男性、もしくは全員女性というのはあ りません。なお、声で男性2人のどちらかを聞き分けなくてはならない、というような設問はなく、 大概名前を呼ぶか、名前を名乗るか何がしか名前に関する言及があるので、その際に誰が何を言った のか、という部分が問われます。なお、3人で話しているので当然会話全体は2往復以上になってい ます。

グラフィック問題とは、会話を聞きながら問題冊子に印刷さ れている表や地図を参照し、その情報についての問いに答え る問題です。なお、このタイプの問題はPart 3の最後の3セッ ト (Questions 62-64, 65-67, 68-70) に登場し、グラフィッ ク情報についての設問はそのセットの中に1問だけ (つまり 3セットで合計3問) あります。また、その際は必ずLook at the graphic.というアナウンスが流れます。その他の2問 (3 セットで6問) は通常のPart 3の問題と変わりはありません。

グラフィックの例：

Department	Floor
Administration	2F
Human Resources	3F
Marketing	4F
Public Relations	5F

Part 3 ● 会話文問題

では会話を聞いて正しい答えをひとつ、選んでみましょう。

⟨23⟩ **Questions 1 through 3 refer to the following conversation.**

❶ What are the speakers mainly discussing?

(A) A road repair　　(B) A TV program

(C) A budget meeting　　(D) An advertisement　　Ⓐ Ⓑ Ⓒ Ⓓ

❷ What does the man say about the branch?

(A) Its location is not so good.　　(B) It has an excellent reputation.

(C) It is located near his home.　　(D) Its manager has been promoted.　　Ⓐ Ⓑ Ⓒ Ⓓ

❸ What is the woman concerned about?

    (A) A busy schedule   (B) The accessibility of some files

    (C) The price of the advertisement   (D) A meeting location   Ⓐ Ⓑ Ⓒ Ⓓ

Questions 4 through 6 refer to the following conversation with chart.

❹ Where does the man most likely work?

    (A) At a furniture store   (B) At a publishing company

    (C) At an accounting firm   (D) At a delivery company   Ⓐ Ⓑ Ⓒ Ⓓ

❺ Look at the graphic. In which department dose Anita Baxter most likely work?

    (A) Administration   (B) Human Resources

    (C) Marketing   (D) Public Relations

    Ⓐ Ⓑ Ⓒ Ⓓ

❻ What will the woman probably do next?

    (A) Review an order form

    (B) Check the inventory

    (C) Contact her colleague

    (D) Meet with a manager   Ⓐ Ⓑ Ⓒ Ⓓ

Department	Floor
Administration	2F
Human Resources	3F
Marketing	4F
Public Relations	5F

Questions 7 through 9 refer to the following conversation with three speakers.

❼ Where does the conversation most likely take place?

    (A) At a factory   (B) At a home improvement store

    (C) At a glass shop   (D) At a construction site   Ⓐ Ⓑ Ⓒ Ⓓ

❽ Why has production been delayed?

    (A) A shipment has not arrived.   (B) A machine is not working properly.

    (C) Some materials have sold out.   (D) Some employees have been out of town.

    Ⓐ Ⓑ Ⓒ Ⓓ

❾ What will the woman most likely do next?

    (A) Meet with a manager   (B) Check the inventory

    (C) Make a reservation   (D) Contact a client   Ⓐ Ⓑ Ⓒ Ⓓ

以下は先の問題のスクリプトです。音声を聞いて空所に入る単語を書き取ってみましょう。また、先の問題が「全体」
問題か「詳細」問題か識別してみましょう。出来たら、ペアで、グループで、同じかどうか確認してみましょう。

Questions 1 through 3 refer to the following conversation.

W: The (   ) we opened on Cunningham Street is not performing as (   ). As
      you have experience in (   ), I was hoping you had some ideas to improve sales.

M: Well, the location is not the best. The ongoing roadworks is taking a lot of traffic
      away from the area. You could be right about that.

W: Have you considered running a series of television commercials? This would help
      customers to (   ) your location.

W: Television? Must be expensive. I'm not sure we could afford it.

M: It's actually more (　　　　) than most people think. Last summer, my agency created a campaign for a local car repair workshop for under $2,500. As a result, their sales tripled during the three weeks the commercial was aired.

❶ (　　　　　　) ❷ (　　　　　　　　) ❸ (　　　　　　　　)

(24) **Questions 4 through 6 refer to the following conversation with chart.**

M: I have a parcel here for Anita Baxter.

W: Sorry, but (　　　　) are now handled by our mail center on the second level.

M: I understand, but I need to receive a (　　　　) from Ms. Baxter for delivery charges.

W: I see. Her office is on the fourth floor...ah... No, actually... she recently changed (　　　　). You'll now find her on the fifth floor. I'll give her a call to let her know you're coming.

M: I'd (　　　　) that. Thank you.

Department	Floor
Administration	2F
Human Resources	3F
Marketing	4F
Public relations	5F
Accounts	6F

❹ (　　　　　　) ❺ (　　　　　) ❻ (　　　　　　)

グラフィック問題は（　　　番）

(25) **Questions 7 through 9 refer to the following conversation with three speakers.**

W : Hi, George and Jason. I heard that our production of windows is (　　　　) schedule here at our factory. Can you tell me what's going on?

M1 : Well, the machine to cut the glass isn't working very well. Jason and me have been trying to (　　　　) it.

M2 : Right. I've examined the machine, and the problem is with its laser cutter. It will take another day to get it fixed.

W : Well, the repair is on top (　　　　). I'll let our clients know that next Monday shipment of windows will be delayed.

❼ (　　　　　　) ❽ (　　　　　) ❾ (　　　　　　)

Exercise Questions! 🚶 »»»

答え合わせが終わったらリスニング力をあげるためにも音読の練習をたくさんしましょう。何度も練習して、スピード、発音、共に問題の音声に近づけることが出来るよう練習しましょう。

More Exercise Questions! 🚶🚶 »»»

ペアで（3人で）会話してみましょう。出来るようになったら、どちらか（誰か）がスクリプトを見ずにアドリブで答えてみましょう。どんな会話になるでしょうか？

📖 Reading ‥‥

Part 7
シングル
パッセージ
-2-

Unit 3ではpart 7のシングルパッセージを学びました。ここでは、Unit 3よりも少し長めの文書やチャット形式の問題を解いてみます。

少し長めの文書であっても、基本的にUnit 3のSPと設問も解き方もあまり大きな違いはありません。ただ、文書が長いので読むことに時間をかけすぎたり、逆に飛ばして読んだりすることのないように気をつけましょう。ですので、設問が3つあったら3分、4つあったら4分のペースは守りながら取り組みましょう。

チャット形式は、スマートフォンでのメッセージや、パソコン上でのチャットのように、二人もしくは複数の人とのやりとりを画面上で読み、答える問題です。若干長めな場合もありますが、飛ばさずに最初から最後まで読むことを忘れないでください。チャットの問題では、Unit 7のリスニングのところで扱う意図問題が必ず1問含まれています。

リスニングとの違いはターゲットとなっている表現を文字で読めるということです。ここでは、At 00:00 A.M., what does the Mr. A mean when he writes, " ... "? のように、「何時何分にAさんが […] と書いた意味は何ですか」という設問の形で出題されます。

Part 7 ● 読解問題

ではPart 7の問題を実際にやってみましょう。制限時間はそれぞれ3分と4分です。

Questions 1-3 refer to the flowing text-massage chain.

Daniel Craig   10:01 A.M.

Hi, Anthony. Can I ask you something? When I tried to log on to my instant messenger, my password was rejected. Actually, my teleconference will start very soon.

Anthony Davis   10:03 A.M.

Didn't you download the newest software? The instant messenger doesn't work without it. My colleague Johnathan Smith, a member of Technical Support department, explained it in the last meeting.

Daniel Craig   10:06 A.M.

Well, I was out of town to meet with my client, and missed it. Can you e-mail me the download instruction?

Anthony Davis   10:08 A.M.

Sure. Got it.

❶ In what department Mr. Davis probably work?

    (A) Information Technology   (B) Technical Support

    (C) Sales   (D) Human Resources   Ⓐ Ⓑ Ⓒ Ⓓ

❷ At 10:06 A.M., what does Mr. Craig most likely mean when he writes, "I was out of town to meet with my client"?

    (A) He was not able to attend the meeting.

    (B) He thought the meeting was canceled.

    (C) He didn't with his colleague.

    (D) He already knew the change.   Ⓐ Ⓑ Ⓒ Ⓓ

❸ What is Mr. Davis asked to do?

    (A) Confirm a reservation   (B) Meet a client

    (C) Attend a meeting   (D) Send an e-mail   Ⓐ Ⓑ Ⓒ Ⓓ

Questions 4-7 refer to the following online chat discussion.

Patrick Chan	9:20 A.M.
Hi, everyone? Phillip Johnson at Johnson Architect will bring the design of the new office building, right?	

David Park	9:21 A.M.
Yes, Patrick. You're right. He will attend the meeting later today.	

Patrick Chan	9:22 A.M.
Our designers and editors are working remotely now, but I don't think we have enough space. I can't wait to see the new building!	

David Park	9:24 A.M.
Yes, we're expanding more than we expected.	

Jessica Whitney	9:26 A.M.
I'm looking forward moving to the new building, too. I'm a bit concerned about our limited budget, though. I know it might be difficult but let's try to keep it within the budget.	

Patrick Chan	9:27 A.M.
Why don't you discuss it at the meeting? Mr. Johnson will attend it.	

David Park	9:28 A.M.
Patrick is right. The architect knows about the budget.	

Jessica Whitney	9:29 A.M.
That's a good idea. I'll bring up the subject at the meeting. I'll send a new agenda by e-mail for everyone.	

❹ Who most likely is Phillip Johnson?

   (A) An author   (B) A designer   (C) An editor   (D) An architect   Ⓐ Ⓑ Ⓒ Ⓓ

❺ At what type of business are the writers most likely involved in?

   (A) A construction company   (B) A publishing company

   (C) A real estate agency   (D) A moving company   Ⓐ Ⓑ Ⓒ Ⓓ

❻ What is true about Ms. Whitney?

   (A) She plans to attend a committee.   (B) She will meet Ms. Johnson for lunch.

   (C) She recently reviewed the design.   (D) She is worried about the cost.

   Ⓐ Ⓑ Ⓒ Ⓓ

❼ At 9:29 A.M., what does Ms. Whitney most likely mean when she writes, "That's a good idea"?

   (A) An item for discussion should be added to the agenda.

   (B) She doubts Johnson Architect meets their needs.

   (C) She will review the new budget proposal by herself.

   (D) A new space will be too expensive.   Ⓐ Ⓑ Ⓒ Ⓓ

Exercise Questions! 🚶 ⟩⟩⟩

前ページでやったパート7の問題を分析してみましょう。どういうタイプの問題だったでしょうか。
「全体」「詳細」「意図問題」から選んで考えてみましょう。

❶ (　　　　　　) ❷ (　　　　　　) ❸ (　　　　　　)

❹ (　　　　　　) ❺ (　　　　　　) ❻ (　　　　　　) ❼ (　　　　　　)

More Exercise Questions! 🚶🚶 ⟩⟩⟩

問題文を使って、今度はもう少し正確に読んでみましょう。ここでは線を引いたり、単語に丸をつけたりしてもかまいません。正解の根拠となる部分をしっかりつかみましょう。終わったら、ペアで、グループで、それらを確認してみましょう。なお、時間は先生の指示に従ってください。

↳ *Review for Today's Lesson*

What did you learn today?

では今日学んだことを自分の言葉でまとめておきましょう。
まとめられたらペアの人と確認してください。

■ リスニングについて
■ リーディングについて
■ 来週までにするべき課題、自分の目標

自分の目標をしっかりペアの人に宣言し終わりましょう。

Part 4-1 | Part 7 DP (Double Passage)

 **Listening** ⋯

Part 4 説明
Part 4はトークを聞いて答える問題です。Unit 1で確認したように、各トークに（　　）つの設問があり、全部で（　　）セット、計（　　）問のパートです。Part 3同様、リスニングなので当然、トークを聞き取る必要があります。ただ、それと同じくらい、設問文や選択肢をあらかじめ読んでおく「先読み」が重要です。

なお、Part 4ではよく出るトークの場面、ポイントがありますのでそれらを確認しておくことも大切な準備です。以下にまとめておきますので、どういうトークがなされそうか、想像してみてください。

問題が読まれる際のQuestion ## through ## refer to the following …の後をしっかり聞き取っておきましょう。
following talk / report / radio broadcast / radio advertisement / telephone message / announcement / tour information / excerpt from a meeting
など、これから流れるトークの内容がある程度予測できます。

トークが流れる場所や場面は、空港や機内 / ラジオ放送 / ラジオ広告 / 会議の一部 (excerpt from a meeting) / 留守番電話 / アナウンス（スーパーや劇場）などです。

Part 4の典型的なトークの流れは、「情報提供 → 次の行動」です。例えば以下のように大まかな流れが決まっています。

● 空港や機内
1. フライトの遅れのお知らせやゲート番号の変更
2. 変更の理由
3. 補償としてのクーポンを受け取る方法や新しいゲートに行くよう指示

● ラジオ放送
1. ある道路が混雑している
2. 交通渋滞の原因
3. 迂回路を通るよう指示

● ラジオ広告
1. よびかけ
2. お得な情報
3. 連絡先

● 会議の一部
1. 新商品の発売について
2. 広告戦略を考えて欲しい
3. グループで意見を出し合うよう指示

● 留守番電話
1. ケータリングサービスから折り返し
2. パーティの人数やメニューを送りました
3. 注文表を送ってくださいと指示

● アナウンス（スーパーや劇場）
1. 本日は特売日です
2. 本日の特売品は野菜や果物です
3. 割引を受けるにはクーポンを提示と指示

このように、情報提供 → 次の行動の指示、という流れを押さえておきましょう。

Part 3同様、設問も2パターンがあり、会話全体のテーマやトピックを尋ねる「全体」問題と、1か所にしか出てこない詳細を尋ねる「詳細」問題があります。よって、問題がどんな情報を聞き取る問題なのかを意識しておくとよいでしょう。

「全体」問題の設問文例：What is the purpose of this talk?
「詳細」問題の設問文例：When will the conference be held?

Part 4 ● トーク問題

ではトークを聞いて正しい答えを選んでみましょう。

◆ ラジオ放送

(26) **Questions 1 through 3 refer to the following radio broadcast.**

❶ What is the main topic of the radio broadcast?
   (A) Business news   (B) A community event
   (C) The weather   (D) Traffic conditions   Ⓐ Ⓑ Ⓒ Ⓓ

❷ What recommendation is made in the broadcast?
   (A) Remaining indoors   (B) Taking an alternate route
   (C) Buying tickets in advance   (D) Visiting a new store   Ⓐ Ⓑ Ⓒ Ⓓ

❸ What will listeners probably hear next?
   (A) A song   (B) A commercial
   (C) A weather forecast   (D) A news report   Ⓐ Ⓑ Ⓒ Ⓓ

◆ 留守番電話

(27) **Questions 4 through 6 refer to the following telephone massage.**

❹ Who is the message most likely intended for?
   (A) A new client   (B) A student
   (C) A hiring manager   (D) A lawyer   Ⓐ Ⓑ Ⓒ Ⓓ

❺ What is the purpose of the call?
   (A) To propose an interview schedule   (B) To apply for a job
   (C) To inquire about an internship   (D) To respond to a request
                                                            Ⓐ Ⓑ Ⓒ Ⓓ

❻ What does the speaker ask the listener to do?
   (A) Bring a résumé   (B) Meet him for lunch
   (C) Call him back   (D) Send him an e-mail   Ⓐ Ⓑ Ⓒ Ⓓ

◆ ラジオ広告

(28) **Questions 7 through 9 refer to the following advertisement.**

❼ What type of business is being advertised?
   (A) An interior design firm   (B) A university
   (C) A software company   (D) A bookstore   Ⓐ Ⓑ Ⓒ Ⓓ

❽ What does the speaker emphasize about the business?
   (A) It is a convenient location.   (B) It has a low price.
   (C) It is environmentally friendly.   (D) It is the most popular in the area.
                                                            Ⓐ Ⓑ Ⓒ Ⓓ

❾ How can listeners get more information?
   (A) By calling the business   (B) By going to the business
   (C) By reading a newsletter   (D) By visiting a Web site   Ⓐ Ⓑ Ⓒ Ⓓ

Exercise Questions! 🚶🚶 »»

以下は先のページの問題のスクリプトです。音声を聞いて空所に入る単語を書き取ってみましょう。また、先ページの問題が「全体」問題か「詳細」問題か識別してみましょう。出来たら、ペアで、グループで、同じかどうか確認してみましょう。

1. ラジオ放送

(26) **Questions 1 through 3 refer to the following radio broadcast.**

Good morning, radio K101 listeners. In traffic news, construction work on the new shopping mall is (　　　　　) heavy traffic delays along El Camino street. To reach the shopping mall between the hours of 10 A.M. and 6 P.M., we (　　　　　) taking Gabriella Road or Dawson Road. For the most (　　　　　) traffic information, (　　　　　) our Web site at www. k101.com. And now, this week's weather outlook.

❶ (　　　　　　　　) ❷ (　　　　　　　　) ❸ (　　　　　　　　)

2. 留守番電話

(27) **Questions 4 through 6 refer to the following telephone massage.**

Hi, this is Clerk Beckham calling from Human Resources of Underwood Law Firm.
I am just giving you a call to (　　　　　) that we received your application form and résumé for our internship program. We were very (　　　　　) by your GPA from your college.
You are (　　　　　) invited to our interview. I will be meeting only with the top candidates to determine who is most (　　　　　) for the internship position.
Would a 1:00 P.M. appointment next Wednesday work for you? I just want to confirm the schedule, so please call me back at 555-0116.
Thanks and have a great day!

❹ (　　　　　　　　) ❺ (　　　　　　　　) ❻ (　　　　　　　　)

3. ラジオ広告

(28) **Questions 7 through 9 refer to the following advertisement.**

Always wanted to get your university degree? What's the hold up? If it's tuition fees, let me tell you. At Yamin's College Institute, we've just discounted the entrance fee by 50%! That's right, it's now officially (　　　　　) to get your university degree, but you've got to do it now! Call before midnight to secure your space in our college program. It just takes one phone call. (　　　　　) this commercial and (　　　　　) an additional 20% off at the campus book store. The number to call is 555-5555. For more details, please (　　　　　) us at yaminscollege.com.
See you this September!

❼ (　　　　　　　　) ❽ (　　　　　　　　) ❾ (　　　　　　　　)

Exercise Questions! 🚶 »»

答え合わせが終わったらリスニング力をあげるためにも音読の練習をたくさんしましょう。基本的に、口に出して「言えない」ものは「聞き取れない」と言われています。何度も練習して、スピード、発音、共に問題の音声に近づけることが出来るよう練習しましょう。

More Exercise Questions! 🚶🚶 »»

ペアの人に向かって、話しかけるようにスクリプトを読んでみましょう。それぞれの状況に応じて、役になりきって読んでみるのが大事です。

📖 Reading ....

Part 7 ダブル パッセージ の特徴	Part 7にはUnit 3で学習したSP（シングルパッセージ）のほかにDP（ダブルパッセージ）と呼ばれる、文書が2つある問題が出題されます。SPと同様、手紙やEメール、記事や広告やお知らせがパッセージに含まれるのは変わりませんが、2つの文書が組み合わさっているのが特徴です。DPは2セット出題され、2セットで合計10問、Questions176-185に割り当てられています。

ただし、DPで注意が必要なのは「2文書型」と呼ばれる問題が出題されることです。1つ目のパッセージと2つ目のパッセージの両方を読まなければ解けない問題を「2文書型」と呼びます。

文書が2つになっても、「1問1分で解く」というスタンスは同じですので、DP2題を10分で解き終わることを目標にしましょう。

設問のタイプはSPと同様、全体を問う問題と詳細を問う問題があります。NOT型問題が出題されるのも同じです。

文書全体の主題、テーマを問う全体問題
例 ▶ What is the article about? / Why was the e-mail sent? /
Why was the letter written?

文書の一部の詳細を問う個別問題
例 ▶ What information does Mr. A want? /
Where does Mr. B work?

文書には書いていないことを問うNOT問題
例 ▶ What is NOT true about ...? /
Who will NOT attend the meeting?

これらの問題に加え、同義語問題（文中の単語と同じ意味の単語を選ぶ問題）が加わります。

文書が2つあったとしても、全ての問いに対して2つの文書を読まなければならない、ということは実はありません。むしろ、2つの文書を参照して内容を確認しなければならない問題は5問中1,2問で、残りの問題はSPと同じアプローチで解けます。

基本的に、最初の問題のヒントは最初のほうに、最後の問題のヒントは最後のほうにある場合が多いことが特徴です。通常、5問あるうちの1問目は1つ目の文書から出題され、主に4,5問目に両文書型が出題されます。

ではPart 7 DPの問題を実際にやってみましょう。制限時間は5分です。

Questions 1-5 refer to the following letter and e-mail.

Sunshine Company
1555 ake Woodlands Avenue
Houston TX, 77045

July 31

I want to make a complaint about Sunshine T241 (serial # 3445HY, red) that I purchased online last week.

Unfortunately, when I received the delivery, the package contained a blue coffee maker, instead of a red one. To resolve this problem I would like you to change the item.

When I first learned of this problem, I contacted Customer Service at your company, and was told that nothing could be done about it. I believe that this response is unfair because my receipts shows that I certainly ordered a red coffee maker. I would like a written statement explaining your company's position and what you will do about my complaint.

I look forward to hearing from you as soon as possible to resolve this problem. I am enclosing copies of my receipt. You can call me at 205-555-0137, or send me an e-mail at racheljones@closemail.com

Sincerely,
Rachel Jones

To:	Rachel Jones <racheljones@closemail.com>
From:	Jonathan Goldsmith <jgoldsmith@sunshinecompany.com>
Subject:	Your order
Date:	August 1

Dear Ms. Jones,

I want to apologize for your inconvenience. Our team tries to offer the best service, but we failed this time. Our Customer Service representative misunderstood our store policy, and we sent the exact item you ordered this morning.

This was likely caused by our new employee, but, regardless, we should have handled this better. We're all aware of what happened and will take extra care in the future. As an additional apology, we're attaching a discount code #77187 for your future purchase. When you check out, simply enter the code, and 15 percent will be taken off your merchandise total. While we know it can't exactly make up for the inconvenience we caused, we hope it'll go some way towards making amends.

Thank you for your patience. Let me know if I can help in any way.

Jonathan Goldsmith
Customer Service Manager

❶ What is indicated about Ms. Jones?

    (A) She is requesting a refund.   (B) She ordered the item in July.

    (C) She chose a blue coffeemaker.

    (D) She has e-mailed the Customer Service before.   Ⓐ Ⓑ Ⓒ Ⓓ

❷ What most likely is the Sunshine T241?

    (A) A microwave oven   (B) A dishwasher

    (C) A coffee maker   (D) A blender   Ⓐ Ⓑ Ⓒ Ⓓ

❸ What is the purpose of the e-mail?

    (A) To announce the release of a new machine

    (B) To provide details about a delivery

    (C) To announce a new policy for returns

    (D) To respond a customer complaint   Ⓐ Ⓑ Ⓒ Ⓓ

❹ What was sent to Ms. Jones in August?

    (A) A red coffee maker   (B) A blue coffee maker

    (C) A drinking water filter   (D) A new cartridge   Ⓐ Ⓑ Ⓒ Ⓓ

❺ What does Sunshine Company offer Ms. Jones?

    (A) A partial refund   (B) A discount on a future purchase

    (C) Complimentary coffee and dessert   (D) Free shipping   Ⓐ Ⓑ Ⓒ Ⓓ

Exercise Questions! 🚶 ››››

左ページでやったパート７の問題を分析してみましょう。どういうタイプの問題だったでしょうか？

❶ (   ) ❷ (   ) ❸ (   )

❹ (   ) ❺ (   )

More Exercise Questions! 🚶🚶 ››››

問題文を使って、今度はもう少し正確に読んでみましょう。ここではスラッシュリーディングをしたり、解答の根拠に線を引いたり、単語に丸をつけたりしてもかまいません。

正解の根拠となる部分をしっかりつかみましょう。終わったら、ペアで、グループで、それらを確認してみましょう。なお、時間は先生の指示に従ってください。

↱ *Review for Today's Lesson*

What did you learn today?

では今日学んだことを自分の言葉でまとめておきましょう。

まとめられたらペアの人と確認してください。

■ リスニングについて

■ リーディングについて

■ **来週までにするべき課題、自分の目標**

自分の目標をしっかりペアの人に宣言し、終わりましょう。

Unit 7

Part 4-2 | Part 7 TP (Triple Passage)

 **Listening** ___

> | グラフィック問題 意図問題 | Unit 6ではPart 4のトーク問題の基本を学びました。このUnitではPart 3にも出題されている形式、グラフィックと意図問題に取り組んでみましょう。 |

グラフィック問題はUnit 5でも取り上げましたが、トークを聞きながら問題冊子に印刷されている表や地図を参照し、その情報についての問いに答える問題です。なお、このタイプの問題はPart 4の最後の2、3セット (Questions 92-94, 95-97, 98-100) に登場し、グラフィック情報についての設問はそのセットの中に1問だけ (つまり2、3セットで合計2、3問) あります。また、その際は必ずLook at the graphic.というアナウンスが流れます。その他の2問 (1セット3問中、グラフィック以外の2問) は通常のPart 4の問題と変わりはありません

グラフィックの例：

Weather Forecast			
Thursday	Friday	Saturday	Sunday
30℃	28℃	32℃	26℃
Cloudy then rain	Sunny	Cloudy	Cloudy with occasional rain

意図問題とは、トークの中で使われた表現がどういう意図を示しているのかを問う問題です。例えば、イベントの紹介がなされているトークで "How could you miss this?" (どうして見逃せるでしょうか？) と言われたら、その真の意図は「ぜひ参加してください」ということになります。このように、意図問題とは言葉の表面的な意味ではなく、言わんとしている意図を正確に把握する問題です。この問題の際には必ず、Why does the speaker say, " …"？、もしくはWhat does the speaker imply when he says, " …"？のような質問文が流れます。

Part 4 ● トーク問題

ではトークを聞いて正しい答えをひとつ、選んでみましょう。

● グラフィック問題 ●

(29) Questions 1 through 3 refer to the following radio broadcast with a table.

Weather Forecast			
Thursday	Friday	Saturday	Sunday
30℃	28℃	32℃	26℃
Cloudy then rain	Sunny	Cloudy	Cloudy with occasional rain

❶ Look at the graphic. What day is it today?

(A) Thursday   (B) Friday

(C) Saturday   (D) Sunday

Ⓐ Ⓑ Ⓒ Ⓓ

❷ What event will take place on Sunday?

(A) A picnic   (B) A parade

(C) An outdoor market   (D) A baseball game

Ⓐ Ⓑ Ⓒ Ⓓ

❸ What does the speaker recommend taking to the event?

(A) A warm coat   (B) A bottle of water

(C) A map   (D) An umbrella

Ⓐ Ⓑ Ⓒ Ⓓ

● 意図問題 ●

(30) Questions 4 through 6 refer to the following telephone message.

❹ Where does the speaker most likely work?

(A) At a government agancy   (B) At an equipment rental store

(C) At a factory   (D) At a shipping company

Ⓐ Ⓑ Ⓒ Ⓓ

❺ What does the man imply when he says, "But, 5000 is a lot"?

(A) He thinks he needs to hire more employees.

(B) He is happy with the order.   (C) It's going to be expensive.

(D) There might be a mistake.

Ⓐ Ⓑ Ⓒ Ⓓ

❻ What is the problem?

(A) Some equipment is not working.

(B) The factory has a limited production capacity.

(C) Merchandise has sold out.

(D) An order has been canceled.

Ⓐ Ⓑ Ⓒ Ⓓ

Exercise Questions! 🚶🚶 ›››

以下は先のページの問題のスクリプトです。音声を聞いて空所に入る単語を書き取ってみましょう。また、先ページの問題が「全体」問題か「詳細」問題か識別してみましょう。出来たら、ペアで、グループで、同じかどうか確認してみましょう。

● グラフィック問題 ●

(29) **Questions 1 through 3 refer to the following radio broadcast with a table.**

Good afternoon, I'm Katarina Heinrich from J102. Welcome to the Katarina's Weather Forecast! Here is today's weather for the British Isles. The Newcastle here will rain this afternoon. It's quite (   ) tomorrow, but the wind is very strong. Be careful! The rain shouldn't (   ) this Saturday's parade. But if you're going to the (   ) international market on Sunday, there is a chance of some rain, so don't (   ) home without your umbrella! On Sunday, the temperature is a bit lower, at around 26°.

❶ (   ) ❷ (   ) ❸ (   )

● 意図問題 ●

(30) **Questions 4 through 6 refer to the following telephone message.**

Hi, Ms. Sparks, I'm (   ) from Hicks Furniture regarding the order you placed last week. Thank you for ordering our new tables. This is the most (   ) table in our company. But, 5000 is a lot. (   ) (   ), Our factory's production capacity is 250 tables a week. Producing 5000 tables (   ) it. Please call me back at 555-0166. I just want to make sure your order. I think one digit too many. Thanks.

❹ (   ) ❺ (   ) ❻ (   )

Exercise Questions! 🚶 ›››

答え合わせが終わったらリスニング力をあげるためにも音読の練習をたくさんしましょう。基本的に、口に出して「言えない」ものは「聞き取れない」と言われています。何度も練習して、スピード、発音、共に問題の音声に近づけることが出来るよう練習しましょう。

More Exercise Questions! 🚶🚶 ›››

ペアの人に向かって、話しかけるようにスクリプトを読んでみましょう。それぞれの状況に応じて、雰囲気を出してみてください。

 **Reading** ⋯

**Part 7
トリプル
パッセージ
の特徴**

Part 7の最後の15題、Questions186-200はTP（トリプルパッセージ）と呼ばれる、文書が3つあるタイプの読解問題です。3つも文書があるので読むのが大変、かつ難しそう、という印象を持つかもしれませんが、文書3つの情報を全て参照しないと答えられない問題は基本的にありません。

1. SPと同様に1つの文書を読めば解ける問題

2. A、B、Cの3つの文書があったとして、AB、BC、ACのいずれか2つの文書を参照すれば解ける問題

このいずれかのパターンで解けるということです。

5問中1, 2問は、これまで同様SPと同じアプローチで解けます。加えて、最初の問題のヒントは最初のほうに、最後の問題のヒントは最後のほうにある場合が多いのもポイントです。

Unit 3でも書きましたが、600-700点を目指す人は、200番まで全て解く必要はありません。最後まで解き終わらずに塗り絵（業界用語で適当に塗ること）をしても良いのです。ただし、だからといってTPのトレーニングをしなくて良い、ということではありません。TPも含めて読解練習をやることで、だんだんスピードがついてきます。

Part 7 ● 読解問題

ではPart 7のTPの問題を実際にやってみましょう。制限時間は5分です。

Questions 1-5 refer to the following advertisement, list, and e-mail.

From the humble beginnings in the back of his parents' restaurant, practicing physician Stephen Young has devoted his life to delivering the best health-promoting products to your door. Over the 35 years Young-life has expanded its line of probiotic drinks to include tea and other energy supplements. But we have never forgotten our founding principle: promoting health and longevity for our customers.

We are now launching a tasty alternative to drinks — a probiotic yogurt. Available in three varieties, our yogurt has all the same healthy bacteria of our drinks and tea. It comes in three delicious varieties for everyone in your family to enjoy. We're sure your children will love the fruit-flavored one.

Young-life products are available in most grocery stores or by delivery. Call 555-1829 to set up delivery for your home or office.

♦ ♦ ♦ Young-life Product List ♦ ♦ ♦

Creamy Drinks		Yogurt		Tea	
#131	Regular (80ml)	#231	Sweetened (80g)	#331	Powerful (110ml)
#132	Low sugar (80ml) **top seller*	#232	Plain (80g)	#332	Ginger (100ml)
#133	Half Calorie (65ml)	#233	Dessert (with fruit) (65g)	#333	Diet (99ml)

To:	Young-life Customer Assistance
From:	Ellen Mayfield
Subject:	My order
Date:	March 26

I am the new office manager at Wilson Architects and I had a question about our standing order. The previous office manager told me that you deliver 30 bottles of your top seller every Monday morning. This past Monday, three days ago, we received 25 bottles. I'm learning a lot of new things at once, so I didn't notice the mistake on the invoice until today. Could you send us the remaining part of our order as soon as possible?

Thank you,

Ellen Mayfield

❶ Who started Young-life?

   (A) A beauty consultant

   (B) A businessperson

   (C) A chef

   (D) A doctor Ⓐ Ⓑ Ⓒ Ⓓ

❷ According to the advertisement, what will children especially enjoy?

   (A) #131   (B) #231

   (C) #233   (D) #332 Ⓐ Ⓑ Ⓒ Ⓓ

❸ What is the largest volume product?

   (A) Diet tea

   (B) Ginger tea

   (C) Powerful tea

   (D) Regular creamy drink Ⓐ Ⓑ Ⓒ Ⓓ

❹ What was missing from Ms. Mayfield's order?

    (A) Half calorie drink

    (B) Low sugar drink

    (C) Plain yogurt

    (D) Sweetened yogurt   Ⓐ Ⓑ Ⓒ Ⓓ

❺ What can be said of Ms. Mayfield?

    (A) She has a new job.

    (B) She has used Young-life products before.

    (C) She is an architect.

    (D) She used to work for Young-life.   Ⓐ Ⓑ Ⓒ Ⓓ

Exercise Questions! 🚶 ⟩⟩⟩

左ページでやったパート７の問題を分析してみましょう。どういうタイプの問題だったでしょうか？

❶ (　　　　　　　) ❷ (　　　　　　　) ❸ (　　　　　　　)

❹ (　　　　　　　) ❺ (　　　　　　　)

More Exercise Questions! 🚶🚶 ⟩⟩⟩

問題文の用紙を使って、今度はもう少し正確に読んでみましょう。ここでは線を引いたり、単語に丸をつけたりしてもかまいません。正解の根拠となる部分をしっかりつかみましょう。終わったら、ペアで、グループで、それらを確認してみましょう。なお、時間は先生の指示に従ってください。

↱ *Review for Today's Lesson*

What did you learn today?

では今日学んだことを自分の言葉でまとめておきましょう。
まとめられたらペアの人と確認してください

■ リスニングについて

■ リーディングについて

■ 来週までにするべき課題、自分の目標

自分の目標をしっかりペアの人に宣言し、終わりましょう。

Unit 8　クォーター模試 / 自己分析

クォーター模試（リスニング25問、リーディング25問）をやってみましょう。時間は30分間です。

問題は先生から配布されますのでそれを使ってください。マークシートはこの本の巻末にあります。

答え合わせをした後、どのパートが出来た／出来なかったのか、自己分析してみましょう。

● **Part 1**　　（　　／2）　　● **Part 5**　　（　　／8）

● **Part 2**　　（　　／8）　　● **Part 6**　　（　　／4）

● **Part 3**　　（　　／9）　　● **Part 7**　　（　　／13）

● **Part 4**　　（　　／6）

● **Listening**　（　　／25）　　● **Reading**　（　　／25）

● **Total**　　（　　／50）

出来たところ、出来なかったところを自分の言葉で以下にまとめてみましょう。

■ リスニング

_____

_____

_____

_____

_____

_____

■ リーディング

_____

_____

_____

_____

_____

_____

■ 今後、学習したいポイント

シートを書き終わったら、ペアで、グループで、その内容を共有して、自分の目標を宣言しましょう。

Part 2 | Part 5

 Listening ⋯

Part 2
復習 Unit 2で学習したPart 2の特徴を復習しましょう。大切なポイントを覚えていますか？
パート2は短い設問文に対する正しい応答を選ぶ問題でした。Unit 1で確認したよう
に、選択肢は（　　）つで、設問、応答、共に印刷されていません。

ではどのようなタイプの設問文があったのか、確認してみましょう。
空所に何が入るか考えてみてください。

● WH疑問文

WHで始まる疑問詞、（　　　　　　　　　　　　　　　　　　　　　）などで始まる疑問文です。この
パターンの場合、最初の（　　　　　）が聞き取れるかどうかで正解できる／できないが決まってしまう
場合が多いので、集中して（　　　　　）を聞くように心がけてください。

● Yes/No 疑問文

答えが（　　　　　　　　）で答えられる、一般的な疑問文パターンです。しかし、Yes / Noと言った
としてもそれだけでは正解にはなりません。Yes / No以下で（　　　　　　　　　　　　）を答えて
いる選択肢は間違いですので、最後まで応答文を聞きましょう。

● 平叙文

クエスチョンマークで終わらない肯定文です。誰かの一言に対して、フォローを入れたり、疑問文で
返すなど、パターンは多岐に渡ります。日本語で、（　　　　　）な会話を思い浮かべてみるとわかり
やすいでしょう。

● 付加疑問文

平叙文の後に isn't it ？や don't you ？のような表現が続き、（　　　　　　　　　）という意味が
付加される疑問文です。頻度はあまり多くはありませんが、出題される疑問文のうちのひとつです。

● 選択疑問文

（　　　　　　　　）を用いてAかBのどちらかを尋ねる、選択式の疑問文です。
1. どちらかを選ぶ　2. どちらでも良い　3. どちらも選ばない
以上3種類が正解のパターンです。

● 否定疑問文

文頭が（　　　　　　　　　　　　　　　　　　　　　）などで始まる疑問文は否定疑問文と呼ばれます。
Yes / Noの返答を日本語で考えると混乱するので、通常の疑問文である "Do you～?" や "Have you
～?" と同様に解けると考えましょう。

パート2では似たような音を含む応答文（選択肢）をわざと用いる、音ワナというひっかけがあります。これは大抵、間違いの選択肢として用意されています。coffee / copy machineのように、なんとなく聞いていると同じ音に聞こえてしまう場合があり、それを根拠に「正解だ！」としないようにしましょう。

Part 2 ● 応答文問題

ではパート2形式の問題をもう一度やってみましょう。Unit 2とは異なる問題です。
設問文のあとに3つの応答文が読まれます。一番適切なものを選びましょう。

(31) ❶ Mark your answer. Ⓐ Ⓑ Ⓒ
(32) ❷ Mark your answer. Ⓐ Ⓑ Ⓒ
(33) ❸ Mark your answer. Ⓐ Ⓑ Ⓒ
(34) ❹ Mark your answer. Ⓐ Ⓑ Ⓒ
(35) ❺ Mark your answer. Ⓐ Ⓑ Ⓒ
(36) ❻ Mark your answer. Ⓐ Ⓑ Ⓒ
(37) ❼ Mark your answer. Ⓐ Ⓑ Ⓒ
(38) ❽ Mark your answer. Ⓐ Ⓑ Ⓒ
(39) ❾ Mark your answer. Ⓐ Ⓑ Ⓒ
(40) ❿ Mark your answer. Ⓐ Ⓑ Ⓒ

Exercise Questions! 🚶

今聞いた音声の大切な部分（文頭やキーワード）だけを聞き取り、書き取ってみましょう。

❶　　　　　　　❷　　　　　　　❸　　　　　　　❹

❺　　　　　　　❻　　　　　　　❼　　　　　　　❽

❾　　　　　　　❿

More Exercise Questions! 🚶🚶

ペアで、グループで比べてみましょう。同じ単語を書き取れていますか？

先ほどの問題を、今度は音声を聞きながら穴埋めしてみましょう。

(31) ❶ (　　　　) will you come to the party?

(A) It was splendid.　　(B) This is my part-time job.　　(C) After the meeting.

Ⓐ Ⓑ Ⓒ

(32) ❷ How many chairs should we (   ) for our guests?

(A) Maybe around 50.   (B) Breads have been prepared for dinner.

(C) I guess Thursday.   Ⓐ Ⓑ Ⓒ

(33) ❸ Would you like another cup of (   )?

(A) Who fixed this copy machine?   (B) I would rather have some tea.

(C) George will do.   Ⓐ Ⓑ Ⓒ

(34) ❹ Do you have time for a quick (   )?

(A) Yes, I have already done it.   (B) During the lunch hour.

(C) Sure, I will go with you.   Ⓐ Ⓑ Ⓒ

(35) ❺ There's a helpful map in this (   ).

(A) OK, I will check it out.   (B) Should we distribute these brochures?

(C) The project has been done.   Ⓐ Ⓑ Ⓒ

(36) ❻ I can't find my (   ) for the next meeting.

(A) I'm meeting a client.   (B) Did you put it on your desk, didn't you?

(B) I wrote it.   Ⓐ Ⓑ Ⓒ

(37) ❼ Our (   ) has been a little delayed, right?

(A) Training is important.   (B) Tomorrow is the best.   (C) Again?   Ⓐ Ⓑ Ⓒ

(38) ❽ You took a (   ) with this author, didn't you?

(A) She'll want to take a picture.   (B) He also gave me his autograph.

(C) Let's pick them up.   Ⓐ Ⓑ Ⓒ

(39) ❾ Which color would you like to have, (   ) or green?

(A) Blue train would be faster.   (B) Do you have a red one?

(C) The blueprints.   Ⓐ Ⓑ Ⓒ

(40) ❿ Aren't you supposed to be on (   ) this weekend?

(A) No, I changed my plan.   (B) A support technician.

(C) He'll be back on Friday.   Ⓐ Ⓑ Ⓒ

Exercise Questions! 🚶🚶 ≫≫≫

正しい応答に○をつけましょう。また、音ワナの箇所に線を引いてみましょう。終わったら、ペアで、グループでくらべてみましょう。

More Exercise Questions! 🚶🚶 ≫≫≫

次に、設問文と正しい応答文を用いて、一問一答形式でお互いに会話してみましょう。
出来るようになったら、今度は応答文を見ないでアドリブで設問に答えてみましょう。

📖 Reading ····

Part 5 復習　Unit 2で学習したPart 5の特徴を復習しましょう。大切なポイントを覚えていますか？
以下の文の空所に入る単語を考えてみましょう。

Part 5は短文穴埋め問題と呼ばれ、空所に単語または句を入れる問題でしたね。

問題は大きくわけで、（　　　　）と（　　　　　）の2種類がありました。文法はその名の通り文法事項に関する問いで、知っていればすぐに解答出来ますが、逆に知らないとその場で解答するのはほぼ不可能です。語彙は単語の（　　　　）が問われているので、こちらも知らなければ基本的にアウトです。言い換えると、このパートは（　　　　）が問われているので、わからなければ（　　　　　）ことがポイントでした。

時間管理が非常に重要で、目安は1問最大で（　　　）秒です。それ以上考えても知らない、わからないと判断したら即座に（　　　　　　　　　　　　　）しましょう。

よって、1問20秒だと3問で（　　　）分、30問出題されるので、全体で（　　　）分でこのパートを駆け抜けるのが理想でしたね。

ただし、設問によっては空所の近くだけを読めば解ける問題もあります。

1. 最初に選択肢をチェック
2. 空所の近くだけを読めば解ける問題かどうかをチェック
   (1) 空所の近くだけを読めば解けそうなら5秒を目安に解く
   (2) 空所の近く以外も読んで解く問題は、20秒以内を目安に解く
3. 知らない問題は捨てる

これを心がけ、トータルで10分以内を目指しましょう。

主に問われる文法事項としては、

品詞（名詞、動詞、形容詞、副詞、単数と複数などの見分け、使い分け）

例 ▶ success / succeed / successful / successfully

動詞の形（時制や態、現在/過去分詞など）

例 ▶ make / makes / made / making / have made / to make

代名詞（格を問う問題）

例 ▶ he / his / him / himself

関係代名詞、関係副詞

例 ▶ that / who / what / which / whose / when / where　など

前置詞

例 ▶ in / on / at / of / with / under / over / along　など

接続詞

例 ▶ once / although / because / while / when　などがありました。

語彙の場合は同じ品詞（名詞、動詞、形容詞、副詞）のものが選択肢に4つ並びます。その中から設問文に入れて意味が通るものを正解に選びます。

品詞問題では、それぞれの接尾辞（語尾）を見ると、ある程度品詞が推測できます。

名　詞：-tion, -sion, -ment, -ty, -ness, -sis, -ance(ence), -cy、人物を表す –er, -or, -ist

例 ▶ information, occasion, agreement, society, teacher, doctor, scientist　など

動　詞：-ize, -fy, -en, -ate

例 ▶ organize, satisfy, fasten, separate など

形容詞：-ous, -ble, -ful, -cal, -tial, -nal, -ive

例 ▶ various, capable, helpful, logical, essential, eternal, positive　など

副　詞：品詞問題では、形容詞＋-ly

例 ▶ variously, capably, helpfully, logically, essentially, eternally, positively　など

ただし、「前置詞vs接続詞」と呼ばれるタイプの問題は、語彙問題ですが文法の知識を使って解きます。例えば as long as（接続詞）/ along with（前置詞）/ however（副詞）/ otherwise（副詞）のような問題です。

この場合は、SVの前には接続詞、名詞の前には前置詞を置きます。

Part 5 ● 文法、語彙問題

Part 5形式の問題をやってみましょう。４つの選択肢の中から一番適切だと思うものを選んでください

❶ A reception to celebrate the ------- of the new restaurant will be held at 7:00 P.M.

(A) opens　(B) open　(C) opening　(D) opened　Ⓐ Ⓑ Ⓒ Ⓓ

❷ The new medication requires government approval ------- it can be sold to consumers.

(A) because of　(B) instead　(C) despite　(D) before　Ⓐ Ⓑ Ⓒ Ⓓ

❸ Dr. Bremen thanked the technicians ------- helped him organize tours of the new laboratory.

(A) who　(B) which　(C) what　(D) whose　Ⓐ Ⓑ Ⓒ Ⓓ

❹ Orders for specialty flower arrangements may ------- over the phone or online.

(A) place　(B) placing　(C) placed　(D) be placed　Ⓐ Ⓑ Ⓒ Ⓓ

❺ *The Sunrise News* is the most widely ------- newspaper in the region.

(A) located　(B) performed　(C) distributed　(D) judged　Ⓐ Ⓑ Ⓒ Ⓓ

❻ Siena Corporation is expanding its office in London and is looking for local sales ------- .

(A) representative　(B) representable　(C) representatives　(D) represents　Ⓐ Ⓑ Ⓒ Ⓓ

❼ Bridgewater Company does not schedule interviews with applicants ------- all recommendation letters have been received.

(A) without　(B) during　(C) until　(D) however　Ⓐ Ⓑ Ⓒ Ⓓ

❽ In ------- current role in new product development for Finch International, Mr. Bauers aims for innovation in new software.

(A) he　(B) him　(C) his　(D) himself　Ⓐ Ⓑ Ⓒ Ⓓ

❾ Horge Packing's shipping ------- are almost impossible to damage and can be opened easily with special tools.

(A) contain　(B) containers　(C) contained　(D) containing　Ⓐ Ⓑ Ⓒ Ⓓ

⓾ For over 30 years, *Journal of Science* ------- a trusted resource for scientists all over the world.

    (A) has been   (B) is   (C) have been   (D) was   Ⓐ Ⓑ Ⓒ Ⓓ

Exercise Questions! 🚶🚶 ⟫⟫⟫

今やった問題を分析してみましょう。（　　　）に文法と語彙のどちらが問われているのか、書いてみましょう。また、その選択肢を選んだ理由も書き出してみましょう。書き終わったら、ペアで、グループで、同じかどうか確認してみましょう。

❶　（　　　　　）　**理由** ▶

❷　（　　　　　）　**理由** ▶

❸　（　　　　　）　**理由** ▶

❹　（　　　　　）　**理由** ▶

❺　（　　　　　）　**理由** ▶

❻　（　　　　　）　**理由** ▶

❼　（　　　　　）　**理由** ▶

❽　（　　　　　）　**理由** ▶

❾　（　　　　　）　**理由** ▶

❿　（　　　　　）　**理由** ▶

More Exercise Questions! 🚶 ⟫⟫⟫

左ページを用いて、設問文を詳しく分析してみましょう。知らない単語は辞書などで調べて意味を書き込んだり、意味のかたまりごとにスラッシュを入れたりして、一文を正確に理解しましょう。

↱ *Review for Today's Lesson*

What did you learn today?

では今日学んだことを自分の言葉でまとめておきましょう。
まとめられたらペアの人と確認してください。

■ リスニングについて

■ リーディングについて

■ 来週までにするべき課題、自分の目標

自分の目標をしっかりペアの人に宣言し、終わりましょう。

Unit 10

本日の学習項目

Part 1 | Part 7 SP (Single Passage)-1

 **Listening** ....

Part 1 復習 写真には大きく分けて4つのパターンがありました。どういう特徴だったでしょうか？ 思い出して書き出してみましょう。書き終わったらペアの人と確認してみましょう。

❶ 人物 (　　　) が写真の中心に写っているもの

→ 人物の動作、何をしているか、(　　　　)、(　　　　　　) などに注意します。

❷ 人物 (　　　　　　　　　　　　) が写真の中心に写っているもの

→ 人物それぞれの動作、何をしているか、2人または3人の (　　　　　)、(　　　　)、(　　　　　) などに注意します。

❸ 人以外の (　　　) が写真の中心に写っているもの　*人物は写っていません。

→ モノがどういう (　　　) にあるのか、に注意します。

❹ (　　　) と (　　　) が一緒に写っているもの

→ どんなモノが写っているのか、(　　　) が何をしているのか、に注意します。

上記4パターンのいずれであっても、(　　　　　　　　　　) ものが正解になることはありません。必ず写っているものに関する英文があるはずですので、それを聞き逃さないようにしましょう。やり方としては以下を参考にしてください。

❶ 写真を見て上記のどのパターンか見分ける。

❷ 写真にどんなものが写っているのか、どんな (　　　) が頭に浮かぶか、を確認する。

❸ 音声をしっかり聞いてマークする。

なお、聞いている間に混乱しないよう、少しでも「そうかな？」と思った選択肢には軽く印をつけておくか、(　　　　　　　　　　) と忘れないでおけるので効果的です。

Exercise Questions! 🚶

以下の単語はパート1に頻出と言われている単語です。いくつ意味を知っていますか？

[utensil / wheelbarrow / canopy / appliance / vehicle / vessel / musical instruments]

More Exercise Questions! 🚶

以下の文章はパート1に頻出と言われている表現を用いた例文です。いくつ意味を知っていますか？

The buildings are reflected on the water.

Electric appliances are unplugged.

Part 1 ● 写真描写問題

4つの音声の中から写真の説明として一番適切なものを選びましょう。

(41) ❶

メモ

Ⓐ Ⓑ Ⓒ Ⓓ

(42) ❷

メモ

Ⓐ Ⓑ Ⓒ Ⓓ

(43) ❸

メモ

Ⓐ Ⓑ Ⓒ Ⓓ

(44) ❹

メモ

Ⓐ Ⓑ Ⓒ Ⓓ

Exercise Questions! 🚶 ›››

前のページの問題のスクリプトです。正解の根拠を確認しましょう。写真の説明として重要な語句に線を引いてみましょう。また、それぞれの選択肢を音読してみましょう。

(41) ❶ (A) She's using a photocopier.
(B) She's pouring some coffee.
(C) She's standing in front of a desk.
(D) She's reading some documents.

(42) ❷ (A) They're talking on the phone.
(B) They're greeting each other.
(C) They're having lunch.
(D) They're sitting on the bench.

(43) ❸ (A) Some chairs are stacked by the wall.
(B) Some paintings are hanging on the wall.
(C) Some people are facing each other.
(D) Some people are sitting side by side.

(44) ❹ (A) Tourists are relaxing on the beach.
(B) Some people are sitting under the umbrellas.
(C) Chairs are unoccupied.
(D) Towels have been spread out on the sand.

 *Exercise Questions!* 🚶🚶 ›››

前のページのメモ欄に、写真に写っているものを英語で書き出してみましょう。終わったらペアでくらべましょう。

📖 Reading ‥‥

Part 7 シングル パッセージ 復習	パート7のシングルパッセージの特徴を復習しましょう。 シングルパッセージは文書が1つだけの問題のパターンです。文書はメール、広告、記事など様々なものがあります。いずれであっても、基本的に文書はすべて読むようにしてください。飛ばし読みなど、一部分しか読まないで問題を解こうとするとかえって情報をうまく掴めず、結果として余計に時間がかかってしまいます。

設問の特徴としては、以下のような設問のパターンがありました。また、主な設問文もありましたね。

文書全体の主題、テーマを問う全体問題
文書の一部の詳細を問う個別問題
文書には書いていないことを問うNOT問題

なお、解く時間の目安は１問１分でした。パート７は全部で54問（問題番号147-200）あるので、このペースでやって54分かかります。公開テストの終了時刻、15時から逆算すると、14時5分にパート７をスタートさせれば、ちょうど15時で終わる計算となります。リーディングは試験時間の管理（タイムマネジメント）がとても大切です。

ただし、600-700点を目指す人は、200番まで全て解く必要はありません。最後まできちんと読んで解く必要があるのは上級者だけです。例えば600点を取るのに必要なリーディグセクション300点を取る場合、最後まで解き終わらずに塗り絵（業界用語で適当に塗ること）をしても良いのです。15問ほど塗り絵をしても、解いた問題を確実に正解できるようにしていけば、300点は取れます

Part 7 ● 読解問題

ではPart 7の問題を実際にやってみましょう。制限時間はそれぞれ２分、２分、３分です。

Questions 1-2 refer to the following e-mail.

To:	alicecook@vemail.com
From:	alambert@lewistechnologies.com
Subject:	Welcome!
Date:	November 22

Dear Ms. Cook,

Welcome aboard! Lewis Technologies is the leading company in automotive industry. We look forward to working with you to help you get the most out of our service.

Here at Lewis Technologies, we are committed to offering high-quality car at affordable prices. We hope that we'll live up to your expectations.

Our excellent customer support team is available 24/7 to help you with any questions. You can contact them at support@lewistechnologies.com or 1-800-555-3541.

Your satisfaction is a priority for us, so feel free to share any feedback you have – we take your opinion seriously and will do our best to implement solutions for you.
Regards,

Adam Lambert
Vice President
Lewis Technologies

❶ Why was the e-mail written?

(A) To celebrate the achievements of the company　(B) To report a problem

(C) To negotiate a contract　(D) To express Mr. Lambert's appreciation

Ⓐ Ⓑ Ⓒ Ⓓ

❷ In the letter, the word "available" in paragraph 3, line 1, is closest in meaning to

(A) free   (B) reasonable   (C) comparable   (D) handful   Ⓐ Ⓑ Ⓒ Ⓓ

Questions 3-4 refer to the following advertisement.

★ ☆ ★ ☆ ★ ☆ ★ ☆ ★ ☆ **Special Offer** ☆ ★ ☆ ★ ☆ ★ ☆ ★ ☆ ★

Monday, November 15

Members of Four Seasons gym can take advantage of a new special offer this winter.

Monthly passes to the Yolanda Tennis Club are available at a 50 percent discount to Four Seasons members.

Passes can be purchased at the gym office, which is open from 10:00 A.M. to 5:00 P.M.

To receive the discount, members must show a valid membership card.

❸ What is being advertised?

(A) A discount on a meal   (B) Passes to a membership
(C) Free tennis lessons   (D) Sports equipment   Ⓐ Ⓑ Ⓒ Ⓓ

❹ What is stated in the advertisement?

(A) Online registration will be available after November 15.
(B) Classes for beginners will be held from Monday to Friday.
(C) Members must show their membership card to receive the discount.
(D) An additional fee is charged for more tennis lessons.   Ⓐ Ⓑ Ⓒ Ⓓ

Questions 5-7 refer to the following e-mail.

To: salesstaff@weiscompany.com
From: marthawillams@weiscompany.com
Date: May 20
Subject: Summer Training Session

Dear Sales Department members,

We wanted to confirm the summer training session for the Sales Department.

Training Session

July 19 – July 21 10:00-17:00, at RST Training Center

Please note that all employees should attend the one-week annual session. Exceptions are generally not made, but please speak to your manager if there is any special circumstance we should consider. All necessary materials and equipment are included in each class.

Lunch will be provided each day, so if you have special dietary requirements, please let me know by e-mail before July 15. There will be a shuttle bus from the headquarters to the Training Center, but you may arrange your own transportation. Please indicate your transportation preference by July 1. I can be reached at marthawillams@weiscompany.com.

Martha Williams
Human Resources Department

❺ What is the purpose of the e-mail?

    (A) To announce an upcoming training session   (B) To publicize a new bus service

    (C) To advertise a department store's sale   (D) Sports equipment

    Ⓐ Ⓑ Ⓒ Ⓓ

❻ When will the event start?

    (A) May 20   (B) July 15   (C) July 19   (D) July 21

    Ⓐ Ⓑ Ⓒ Ⓓ

❼ What is NOT included in the training?

    (A) Online tutorials   (B) Equipment   (C) Textbooks   (D) Lunch

    Ⓐ Ⓑ Ⓒ Ⓓ

Exercise Questions! 🚶

前ページでやったパート7の問題を分析してみましょう。どういうタイプの問題だったでしょうか？

❶（　　　　）❷（　　　　）

❸（　　　　）❹（　　　　）

❺（　　　　）❻（　　　　）❼（　　　　）

More Exercise Questions! 🚶🚶

問題文を使って、今度はもう少し正確に読んでみましょう。ここでは線を引いたり、単語に丸をつけたりしてもかまいません。正解の根拠となる部分をしっかりつかみましょう。終わったら、ペアで、グループで、それらを確認してみましょう。なお、時間は先生の指示に従ってください。

《文書のまとめ》前ページの文書がどういう内容であったか、それぞれ簡単にまとめましょう。

↻ *Review for Today's Lesson*

What did you learn today?

では今日学んだことを自分の言葉でまとめておきましょう。
まとめられたらペアの人と確認してください。

■ リスニングについて

■ リーディングについて

■ 来週までにするべき課題、自分の目標

自分の目標をしっかりペアの人に宣言し、終わりましょう。

本日の学習項目

Part 3-1 | Part 6

 **Listening** ….

Part 3 復習

Part 3は（　　　　）を聞いて答える問題でした。Unit 1で確認したように、各会話文に（　　　）つの設問があり、全部で（　　　）セット、計（　　　）問のセクションです。リスニングなので当然、会話が聞き取れないといけないのですが、それと同じくらい問題を解く際に重要なことがありました。それは設問文や選択肢を、会話を聞く前に読んでおく「（先読み）」と呼ばれるテクニックです。

先読みは、「疑問詞、主語、キーワード」を意識して読むようにしましょう。特にPart 3の場合は、「男性」「女性」のどちらのセリフなのかを意識するだけでも、ぐっと聞き取りやすくなります。

例えば

　　　What will the man probably do next?　/　Why is the man concerned?

という設問では、「これから○○します」あるいは「○○が心配です」という発言主は男性です。

先に問題文を読んでおくことで、これから流れる会話が聞きやすくなりますが、ただ読むだけでは効果がありません。先に読んで「準備をする」という意識が大切です。
つまり、（　　　　　　）とは「知りたい情報、知らないといけない情報とは何か」を把握することなのです。よって、問題（　　　　　　）→ リスニング → 解答する、のリズムを体内に感覚として作っておくことが肝心です。

なお、Part 3ではよく出る会話の場面、ポイントもありました。Unit 4を参考に、どういう場面が頻出の場面だったか書き出してみましょう。また、そこでどういう会話がなされそうか想像して、ペアの人と比べてみましょう。

　　　　　　　　　　　　／　　　　　　　／　　　　　　　／　　　　　　　／

A → B → A → Bの2往復の会話が典型的なパターンですが、2.5往復や3往復の場合もあります。いずれにしても、「問題 → 解決」が基本的なパターンです。そして、1セットの会話（時間にして40秒ほど）で、問題は必ず解決します。

設問の種類も（　　）パターンがあり、会話全体のテーマやトピックを尋ねる「（　　）」問題と、1か所にしか出てこない詳細を尋ねる「（　　）」問題がありました。

　　「（　　）」問題の設問文例：（　　　　　　　　　　　　　　　　　　　　　　　）
　　「（　　）」問題の設問文例：（　　　　　　　　　　　　　　　　　　　　　　　）

Part 3 ● 会話文問題

では会話を聞いて正しい答えをひとつ、選んでみましょう。

(45) **Questions 1 through 3 refer to the following conversation.**

❶ What are the speakers discussing?
(A) A book title   (B) A magazine article
(C) A cover design   (D) A bookstore   Ⓐ Ⓑ Ⓒ Ⓓ

❷ Why is the woman concerned?
(A) The title is hard to read.   (B) An order is incorrect.
(C) The schedule needs to be revised.   (D) An event has been canceled.
Ⓐ Ⓑ Ⓒ Ⓓ

❸ What does the woman say she will do?
(A) Arrange an interview   (B) Make a phone call
(C) Find a photograph   (D) Send an e-mail   Ⓐ Ⓑ Ⓒ Ⓓ

(46) **Questions 4 through 6 refer to the following conversation.**

❹ Who is the woman?
(A) An editor   (B) A radio broadcaster
(C) A professor   (D) A nurse   Ⓐ Ⓑ Ⓒ Ⓓ

❺ What has Dr. Feldman recently done?
(A) Opened a new clinic   (B) Given a presentation
(C) Written a book   (D) Won a prize   Ⓐ Ⓑ Ⓒ Ⓓ

❻ What is special about Dr. Feldman's tips?
(A) They are for adults.   (B) They are used with some tools.
(C) They are introduced for the first time.   (D) They are easy to use.   Ⓐ Ⓑ Ⓒ Ⓓ

(47) **Questions 7 through 9 refer to the following conversation.**

❼ Why does the woman want to change her tickets?
(A) She needs time to buy some gifts.   (B) She wants to upgrade her seat.
(C) She has the wrong ticket.   (D) She arrived at the station early.   Ⓐ Ⓑ Ⓒ Ⓓ

❽ What does the man suggest the woman to do?
(A) Receive a full refund   (B) Buy an additional ticket
(C) Speak with a supervisor   (D) Change the destination   Ⓐ Ⓑ Ⓒ Ⓓ

❾ What does the man say about the express train?
(A) It is fully booked.   (B) It will not stop Boston.
(C) It will depart soon.   (D) t costs more.   Ⓐ Ⓑ Ⓒ Ⓓ

Exercise Questions! 🚶🚶 >>>

以下は先の問題のスクリプトです。音声を聞いて空所に入る単語を書き取ってみましょう。また、先の問題が「全体」問題か「個別」問題か識別してみましょう。出来たら、ペアで、グループで、同じかどうか確認してみましょう。

(45) **Questions 1 through 3 refer to the following conversation.**

M: Hi, Diana. I just e-mailed you a file of the cover (   ) for the cookbook. Could you (   )(   )(   ) at it and give me some feedback?

W: Yes, I was just looking at it only a few minutes ago. I really like the (   ) that you chose for the cover, but I am (   ) about the font of the title. I think It's a bit hard to read.

M: Well, I guess you're right. Any thoughts that I should use (   )(   ) it?

W: I'll e-mail you a few (   ).

❶ (   ) ❷ (   ) ❸ (   )

(46) **Questions 4 through 6 refer to the following conversation.**

W: Good morning. I'm Samantha Anderson. You're listening to Health Tips on Radio 101. Welcome, Dr. Feldman. It's a (   ) to have you on the program today.

M: Thank you, Samantha. I'm happy to be here to talk about my new book "*Best Sleep.*" Sleep is important for your health. You can't (   ) on your job or study if you don't get enough sleep. Actually, sleep is the best (   ).

W: Actually, I haven't been sleeping well lately. Do you have some tips for a good night's sleep?

M: Well, I wrote three (   ) in this book. Appropriate room temperature, darkness, and routine before bedtime. The tips are very simple, and easy. I'll talk about one of the tips, "darkness" today.

❹ (   ) ❺ (   ) ❻ (   )

(47) **Questions 7 through 9 refer to the following conversation.**

W: Excuse me. I have a (   ) ticket to New York, but I need a ticket to Boston. It seems that I accidentally bought the wrong ticket, so I'd like to get a refund.

M: That (   ) all the time. We can offer you a refund, but we also can change the destination. Why don't you change it? It's easier and (   ) to process. There is a $5 service charge for changing the ticket, though.

W: Oh, five dollars? That's no problem. I'll change my ticket. I was hoping I could get on an express train. Is that (   )?

M: Sure. There's an express train to Boston in ten minutes. Here's your new ticket.

❼ (   ) ❽ (   ) ❾ (   )

More **Exercise Questions!** 🚶

答え合わせが終わったらリスニング力をあげるためにも音読の練習をたくさんしましょう。何度も練習して、スピード、発音、共に問題の音声に近づけることが出来るよう練習しましょう。

More & More **Exercise Questions!** 🚶🚶

ペアで会話してみましょう。出来るようになったら、どちらかがスクリプトを見ずにアドリブで答えてみましょう。どんな会話になるでしょうか？

Reading ....

Part 6 復習

空所に当てはまる単語を入れながらPart 6について確認しましょう。

Part 6は文書を読み、空所に適切な語（　　）または文を入れる問題です。1文書に対して（　　）問、（　　）文書あるので合計（　　）問の設問が出題されます。

時間配分としては1問（　　）秒、つまり1文書に約（　　）分、Part 6全体で約（　　）分が理想の解答時間です。先に学習したPart 5が約（　　）分でしたので、おおまかに言うとPart 5, 6で合計約（　　）分。公開テストにおいては、リスニング終了後すぐ、13時45分頃からリーディングセクションをスタートすると、約（　　）分後の（　　）時（　　）分までにこの2パートを終えられるのが理想です。

さて、Part 6には2つのタイプの設問、（　　）型と（　　）型、が存在します。（　　）型とは、文書の流れを必ずしも理解する必要はなく、該当する一文のみをしっかり見れば解ける問題、いわば形を変えたPart（　　）でした。文法を問われることが多いので、先にやった（　　）、（　　）の見極めがここで生きてきます。（　　）型はその逆で、文書の流れがわかっていないと答えられない問題です。この場合は少なくとも前後の（　　）文の流れが掴めないと手がかりを得ることが出来ません。その究極の形が文挿入問題で、一文まるごと正しい文を入れないといけないので、初級者には手ごわい問題でしょう。なお、この文挿入問題はその該当箇所が文頭、文中、文尾のどこであれ、他の問題を解き終わった（　　）にやることがポイントでしたね。

■ タイムマネジメントのまとめ

13:00	リスニング	
13:45	Part 5（　　題）＋Part 6（　　題）	
（　　）:（　　）	Part 7（　　題）	
15:00		

Part 6 ● 文法、語彙、文脈理解問題

ではPart 6の問題を実際にやってみましょう。

Questions 1-4 refer to the following advertisement.

☺ Gokey Amusement Park ☺

63 S. Main St., Los Angeles, CA 90210

Phone: (328) 555-5112

info@gokeyamusementpark.com

---**1.**--- you have children or are just a child at heart, visit Gokey Amusement Park and experience one of America's oldest hand-carved wooden carousels. Built ---**2.**--- the city planners between 1854 and 1856, the Gokey Carrousel was completely renovated in 1973 and repainted in 1990. The Hartsfield Carrousel ---**3.**--- 25 horses and 21 menagerie figures, including 5 bears, 4 ostriches, 3 cats, 3 rabbits, and a seahorse. ---**4.**---.

Adults: *$2 per ride*
Seniors: *$1 per ride*
Children over 3: *$1 per ride*
Children 3 and under: *Free*

◎ **Hours** ◎
Monday to Friday 9 A.M. - 5:30 P.M.
Saturday and Sunday 9 A.M. – 7 P.M.

❶ (A) But also (B) Whether (C) Neither (D) Either   Ⓐ Ⓑ Ⓒ Ⓓ

❷ (A) at (B) on (C) by (D) from   Ⓐ Ⓑ Ⓒ Ⓓ

❸ (A) will feature (B) features (C) was featured (D) will be featured   Ⓐ Ⓑ Ⓒ Ⓓ

❹ (A) In other words, regardless of your tastes, there's an animal for you.

   (B) This rule also applies to individuals who may wish to visit the amusement park.

   (C) Therefore, Gokey Amusement Park's official tours are offered seven days a week.

   (D) However, Gokey Amusement Park offers a range of musical entertainment.

    Ⓐ Ⓑ Ⓒ Ⓓ

Questions 5-8 refer to the following e-mail.

To:	All employees
From:	Casey James [cjames@allenconpany.com]
Subject:	Retirement
Date:	October 31

Dear colleagues,

I know you have all heard I decided to retire. ---**5.**---. I am looking forward to my new life of leisure, but of course, I am a little saddened by the thought of not seeing all of you every day. I was very fortunate ---**6.**--- to many global projects, where I had the honor of working with wonderful coworkers like you. Over the years, I have learned something valuable from each of ---**7.**---. I will take all my ---**8.**--- as an asset to guide me through difficult times that may come up in the future.

I am leaving the organization, but I am taking your friendship with me. Please keep in touch. You all have my cell phone number, (800)-324-5555; please feel free to use it. Thank you and best wishes to all of you!

Sincerely,
Casey James

❺ (A) First of all, I am now planning to relocate to the eastern part of the city.

   (B) Today is my last day at Allen Company and I would like to reach out to everyone to say thank you.

   (C) Steve Sanders, our head of Human Resources, will be in touch soon with all the necessary documents you will need to fill out.

   (D) Congratulations on your new job here as a new global project. Ⓐ Ⓑ Ⓒ Ⓓ

❻ (A) assign　(B) assigned　(C) to be assigned　(D) to assign　　Ⓐ Ⓑ Ⓒ Ⓓ

❼ (A) him　(B) them　(C) her　(D) you　　Ⓐ Ⓑ Ⓒ Ⓓ

❽ (A) experiences　(B) holdings　(C) responsibilities　(D) services　　Ⓐ Ⓑ Ⓒ Ⓓ

Exercise Questions! 🚶🚶 »»»

ここでは今やった問題を分析してみましょう。（　　　）に独立型と文脈型のいずれであるのか、書いてみましょう。また、その選択肢を選んだ理由も書き出してみましょう。書き終わったら、ペアで、グループで、同じかどうか確認してみましょう。

❶ (　　　) **理由** ▶

❷ (　　　) **理由** ▶

❸ (　　　) **理由** ▶

❹ (　　　) **理由** ▶

❺ (　　　) **理由** ▶

❻ (　　　) **理由** ▶

❼ (　　　) **理由** ▶

❽ (　　　) **理由** ▶

*More **Exercise Questions!*** 🚶 »»»

前ページを用いて、文書を詳しく分析してみましょう。知らない単語は辞書などで調べて意味を書き込んだり、意味のかたまりごとにスラッシュを入れたりして、一文を正確に理解しましょう。

↳ *Review for Today's Lesson*

What did you learn today?

では今日学んだことを自分の言葉でまとめておきましょう。
まとめられたらペアの人と確認してください。

■ リスニングについて

■ リーディングについて

■ 来週までにするべき課題、自分の目標

自分の目標をしっかりペアの人に宣言し、終わりましょう。

Unit 12

Part 3-2 | Part 7 SP (Single Passage) -2

 **Listening** ·····

Part 3 -2復習

Unit 11ではPart 3の基本的なパターン、パートの概要を復習しました。このUnitではPart 3の中でも若干難易度が高い、あるいは一見複雑そうな問題を再び扱います。Part 3の基本形、A → B → A → Bの2往復以外のパターンとして以下のものがありました。

長めの会話 ／ 3人の会話 ／ グラフィック ／
意図問題（この問題についてはPart 4、Part 7のところで解説しました。）

長めの会話とは、A → B → A → Bのあとにさらに会話が続き、結果として3往復以上になっているものを指しました。この場合はやりとりが長くなっただけで、設問で問われる内容は2往復のものと何ら変わりはありません。

3人の会話とは、A、Bだけでなくcも登場し、3人で話が進行する状況でした。大抵、男性2人と女性1人、あるいは女性2人と男性1人からなっていて、全員男性、もしくは全員女性というのはほとんどありませんでした。なお、声で男性2人のどちらかを聞き分けなくてはならない、というような設問はなく、大概名前を呼ぶか、名前を名乗るかなど名前に関する言及があるので、その際に誰が何を言ったのか、という部分が問われます。なお、3人で話しているので当然会話全体は2往復以上になっています。

また、3人の会話のようにQuestions # through # refer to the following conversation with three speakers.と、最初の問題番号のところをしっかり聞いていれば、3人の会話問題だとあらかじめ予測できます。

グラフィック問題とは、会話を聞きながら問題冊子に印刷されている表や地図を参照し、その情報についての問いに答える問題でした。なお、このタイプの問題はPart 3の最後の3セット（Questions 62-64, 65-67, 68-70）に登場し、グラフィック情報についての設問はそのセットの中に1問だけ（つまり3セットで合計3問）あります。また、その際は必ずLook at the graphic.というアナウンスが流れ、その他の2問（3セットで6問）は通常のPart 3の問題と変わりはありません。

Part 3 ● 会話文問題

では会話を聞いて正しい答えをひとつ、選んでみましょう。

◆ 3人の会話

(48) **Questions 1 through 3 refer to the following conversation with three speakers.**

❶ What problem does the woman mention?

(A) She cannot use the wireless network.　(B) She cannot print some documents.

(C) She cannot make a phone call.　(D) She cannot attend a meeting.

Ⓐ Ⓑ Ⓒ Ⓓ

❷ What has caused the problem?

(A) An electricity failure　(B) A computer malfunction

(C) Maintenance work　(D) A billing error

Ⓐ Ⓑ Ⓒ Ⓓ

❸ What will the woman do this afternoon?

(A) Attend a meeting　(B) Create a document

(C) Fix a computer　(D) Purchase some equipment

Ⓐ Ⓑ Ⓒ Ⓓ

◆ 長めの会話

(49) **Questions 4 through 6 refer to the following conversation.**

❹ Who most likely is the man?

    (A) A store manager   (B) A restaurant owner

    (C) A hotel employee   (D) A safety inspector   Ⓐ Ⓑ Ⓒ Ⓓ

❺ What does the man ask the woman to do?

    (A) Rearrange her schedule   (B) Review a document

    (C) Fill out a customer satisfaction form   (D) Prepare a tag   Ⓐ Ⓑ Ⓒ Ⓓ

❻ What will the woman probably do next?

    (A) Check a Web site   (B) Go to the top floor

    (C) Make a phone call   (D) Return a key   Ⓐ Ⓑ Ⓒ Ⓓ

(50) **Questions 7 through 9 refer to the following conversation and building directory.**

● グラフィック問題 ●

❼ Look at the graphic. Where most likely are the speakers?

    (A) Suite 110   (B) Suite 120

    (C) Suite 130   (D) Suite 140   Ⓐ Ⓑ Ⓒ Ⓓ

❽ What does the man say he wants to do?

    (A) Change a color   (B) Buy a different item

    (C) Get a refund   (D) Return an unwanted item   Ⓐ Ⓑ Ⓒ Ⓓ

❾ What problem does the woman mention?

    (A) An item is out of stock.

    (B) A shop is about to close.

    (C) Price have recently increased.

    (D) A manager is not available.   Ⓐ Ⓑ Ⓒ Ⓓ

Building Directory

South Entrance	
Eggs Restaurant	Suite 110
DDM Shoes	Suite 120
Bell Clothing	Suite 130
Silver Flowers	Suite 140

以下は先の問題のスクリプトです。音声を聞いて空所に入る単語を書き取ってみましょう。また、先の問題が「全体」問題か「個別」問題か識別してみましょう。出来たら、ペアで、グループで、同じかどうか確認してみましょう。

(48) **Questions 1 through 3 refer to the following conversation with three speakers.**

W: Rick, could you help me? I can't print my document on the network printer.

M1: OK. Let me try printing on my computer…Hmm…I can't do it, either. Oh, hi, John, you came at (   ) (   ) (   ) (   ). Could you help us?

M2: Hi. What (   ) (   ) (   ) the problem?

M1: She can't print her documents on the network printer, John.

M2: The network printing service is now under (   ). You can't use the printer until the work is finished.

W: Oh, no. I have to print this document as soon as possible. I have a meeting with my (   ) (   ) this afternoon.

M2: No problem. The maintenance work will be finished by 11 A.M., so you can print your document before the meeting.

❶ (　　　　　　　　) ❷ (　　　　　　　　) ❸ (　　　　　　　　)

(49) **Questions 4 through 6 refer to the following conversation.**

M: Welcome to the Martin Hotel. May I help you?

W: I'd like to (　　　)(　　　). My name is Laura Smith. This is my confirmation slip.

M: Ms. Smith. Yes, we have your reservation. (　　　), your room won't be (　　) until 2:00 P.M.

W: No problem. I just flew in from Vancouver for a conference. I'd like to see some of the city's attractions. Can you keep my luggage at this desk?

M: Certainly. Could you write down your name on this identification tag? We'll put it on your (　　　).

W: Thank you. By the way, Do you have any (　　　　) for good restaurants in the area? I'd like to have lunch before (　　　).

M: You can have lunch at our restaurant on the top floor.

W: That's a good idea.

❹ (　　　　　　) ❺ (　　　　　　) ❻ (　　　　　　　)

(50) **Questions 7 through 9 refer to the following conversation and building directory.**

M: Excuse me, I saw your (　　　　), and bought this red shirt.

W: Thank you for shopping with us. How may I help you today?

M: Well, I really like this shirt, and want to buy a different one. Do you have any other (　　)(　　　) for this item? I wear a medium size.

W: I'm sorry, we're sold out of them. This shirt has been very (　　　) this season. Can I show you some other shirts?

M: I think I'll look (　　) a bit more, thanks.

❼ (　　　　　　) ❽ (　　　　　　) ❾ (　　　　　　　)

Exercise Questions! 人 ››››

答え合わせが終わったらリスニング力をあげるためにも音読の練習をたくさんしましょう。基本的に、口に出して「言えない」ものは「聞き取れない」と言われています。何度も練習して、スピード、発音、共に問題の音声に近づけることが出来るよう練習しましょう。

More Exercise Questions! 人人 ››››

ペア（3人）の人に向かって、話しかけるようにスクリプトを読んでみましょう。それぞれの状況に応じて、雰囲気を出してみてください。

📖 Reading ····

Part 7 シングル パッセージ -2-

Unit 10ではpart 7のシングルパッセージを復習しました。ここでは、Unit 5でも学習したチャット形式の問題を再び取り扱います。Unit 10よりも少し長めの文書や、長めのチャット形式の問題を解いてみます。

少し長めの文書であっても、基本的にUnit 3,5のSPと設問も解き方もあまり大きな違いはありません。ただ、文書が長いので読むことに時間をかけすぎたり、逆に飛ばして読んだりすることのないように気をつけましょう。ですので、設問が3つあったら3分、4つあったら4分、のペースは守りながら取り組みましょう。

チャット形式は、スマートフォンでのメッセージや、パソコン上でのチャットのように、二人もしくは複数の人のやりとりを画面上で読み、答える問題です。若干長めな場合もありますが、飛ばさずに最初から最後まで読むことを忘れないでください。チャットの問題では、Unit 7のリスニングのところで扱う意図問題が必ず1問含まれています。

また、位置選択問題という出題形式もあります。文書中の4つの空所の中から、設問の文を挿入して文意の通る位置を選ぶ問題です。位置選択問題は必ずセットの最後の問題として出題されます。英文には、「1つの段落には1つの話題」というルールがありますので、最後まできちんと読めていれば、セットの最後の位置選択問題は解きやすくなります。

リスニングとの違いはターゲットとなっている表現を文字で読めるということです。ここでは、At 00:00 A.M., what does Mr. A mean when he writes, " ... "? のように、「何時何分にAさんが[…]と書いた意味は何ですか」という設問の形で出題されます。

Part 7 ● 読解問題

ではPart 7の問題を実際にやってみましょう。制限時間はそれぞれ3分、3分、3分です。

Questions 1-3 refer to the following Web page.

JOB Openings 》》》

Liverpool Medical Centre (LMC) are looking for a 2 part-time Receptionists (minimum 15 hours) to join our busy team based close to the city centre of Liverpool. You will be the first point of contact for our patients telephoning or coming in to the Medical Center. The successful candidate will enjoy working as part of a friendly, dedicated team, with the added satisfaction of working for an organization committed to the care and wellbeing of others.

Previous experience of working in medical institutions is desirable although not essential as full training in reception and administrative duties will be provided. Knowledge/experience of Integrated Clinic System is desirable although again not essential.

The salary is £9.00 per hour depending on experience.

Please note that this vacancy may close before the advertised closing date if sufficiently suitable applications are received.

Apply on our employer's Web site >>> click here

❶ What duty is mentioned as part of the job?

    (A) Receiving calls from medical representatives

    (B) Meeting patients coming in to the medical facility

    (C) Working only during night shifts

    (D) Calling people who are unfamiliar with the clinic   Ⓐ Ⓑ Ⓒ Ⓓ

❷ According to the advertisement, what is a requirement for applicants?

    (A) Computer Skills   (B) Previous medical experience

    (C) Coursework in medicine   (D) Communication with a team   Ⓐ Ⓑ Ⓒ Ⓓ

❸ According to the advertisement, why should applicants visit the LMC Web site?

    (A) To apply for the receptionist job (B) To learn about LMS employees

    (C) To request information about the job (D) To ask questions about the process

                                                      Ⓐ Ⓑ Ⓒ Ⓓ

Questions 4-6 refer to the following online chat discussion.

Charlie Paterson 10:20 A.M.
Hi, Olivia. Can I have some questions?

Olivia Carson 10:22 A.M.
Sure. What's happened?

Charlie Paterson 10:24 A.M.
I'm in our warehouse, and checked the inventory. Garcia Olive Oil is currently out of stock. Did you order additional bottles? Brown Italian needs some bottles.

Olivia Carson 10:25 A.M.
Actually, we had a meeting last week, and we decide to replace some items. Our buyer found a new, reliable brand. We're going to offer Miller Olive Oil. You can find them in the middle of the aisle 3.

Charlie Paterson 10:28 A.M.
Oh, I was on vacation and didn't know the decision. OK. I found them. Do all restaurants know about the change? Can I send Brown Italian the new brand oil?

Olivia Carson 10:29 A.M.
Yes. I e-mailed all of the restaurant. I send some samples to all of the restaurant, and they like Miller Olive Oil.

Charlie Paterson 10:30 A.M.
All right. Thanks.

❹ What kind of business do the writers most likely work?

    (A) A hotel

    (B) A coffee shop

    (C) A botanical garden

    (D) A food supplier

    Ⓐ Ⓑ Ⓒ Ⓓ

❺ At 10:22 A.M. what does Ms. Carson most likely mean when she writes, "Sure"?

    (A) She can order some more olive oil.

    (B) She understands the client's concern.

    (C) She is ready to answer the questions.

    (D) She agrees to have a meeting.

    Ⓐ Ⓑ Ⓒ Ⓓ

❻ What is indicated about Mr. Paterson?

    (A) He took some time off recently.

    (B) He works as a delivery driver.

    (C) He sent some e-mails for his client.

    (D) He has a meeting with a client.

    Ⓐ Ⓑ Ⓒ Ⓓ

Questions 7-9 refer to the following e-mail.

To:	Thomas Taylor <ttaylor@greenline.com>
From:	Megan Anderson <megananderson@cmail.com>
Subject:	Job interview
Date:	August 2

Dear Mr. Taylor

I just wanted to thank you for inviting me to your office yesterday. [1] It was great to hear about Greenline's goals for streamlining its software by placing an emphasis on the EX7000 design, and how you see the engineering department playing a role in these initiatives. To follow up on our conversation about the new Web site, I've attached a file in which I summerized my initial ideas. [2]

As I mentioned yesterday, I am a graphic designer at NT design, and I believe that my ten-year experience there makes me well suited for the Web designer position at your company. Greenline seems like a wonderful place to work --- and not just because you mentioned some great summer outings! [3] I really admire the mission that drives your business, and look forward to the opportunity of working with your team to implement some of the ideas I mentioned about redesigning the Web site. [4]

For the last year, I have been a graphic designer for a local accounting firm, where I was responsible for designing the company's Web site

Please let me know if there's anything else you need from me to move the process forward.

Sincerely,
Megan Anderson

❼ Why was the e-mail written?
(A) To describe job qualifications   (B) To submit a job application
(C) To thank for a job interview   (D) To accept a job offer

Ⓐ Ⓑ Ⓒ Ⓓ

❽ How long has Ms. Anderson been at her current position?
(A) Ten months   (B) One year   (C) Three years   (D) Ten years

Ⓐ Ⓑ Ⓒ Ⓓ

❾ In which of the positions marked [1], [2], [3], and [4] does the following sentence best belong?
"I'd be happy to discuss the contents further if you see it being a helpful resource."
(A) [1]   (B) [2]   (C) [3]   (D) [4]

Ⓐ Ⓑ Ⓒ Ⓓ

Exercise Questions! 🚶 ⟫⟫⟫

前ページでやったパート7の問題を分析してみましょう。どういうタイプの問題だったでしょうか？

❶ (   ) ❷ (   ) ❸ (   )
❹ (   ) ❺ (   ) ❻ (   )
❼ (   ) ❽ (   ) ❾ (   )

More Exercise Questions! 🚶🚶 ⟫⟫⟫

問題文を使って、今度はもう少し正確に読んでみましょう。ここでは線を引いたり、単語に丸をつけたりしてもかまいません。正解の根拠となる部分をしっかりつかみましょう。終わったら、ペアで、グループで、それらを確認してみましょう。なお、時間は先生の指示に従ってください。

↳ *Review for Today's Lesson*

What did you learn today?

では今日学んだことを自分の言葉でまとめておきましょう。
■リスニングについて　■リーディングについて　■来週までにするべき課題、自分の目標
ペアで（グループで）上に書いた内容を共有し、自分の目標をしっかり宣言しましょう。

Unit 13

本日の学習項目

Part 4-1 | Part 7 DP (Double Passage)

Listening ⋯

Part 4 復習
Part 4はトークを聞いて答える問題でしたね。Unit 1で確認したように、各トークに（　　）つの設問があり、全部で（　　）セット、計（　　）問のパートでした。Part 3同様、リスニングなので当然、トークが聞き取れないといけないのですが、それと同じくらい、問題を解く際には設問文や選択肢を聞く前に読んでおく「（先読み）」が重要です。

なお、Part 4ではよく出るトークの場面、ポイントがありますのでそれらをあらかじめ知っておくことも大切な準備でした。以下にそうした場面を書き出して、どういうトークがなされそうか、想像してみてください。

問題が読まれる際のQuestion ## through ## refer to the following …の後をしっかり聞き取っておきましょう。
following talk / report / radio broadcast / telephone message / announcement / tour information / excerpt from a meeting
など、これから流れるトークの内容がある程度予測できます。

Unit 6を参照しながら、穴埋めしましょう。
トークが流れる場所や場面は、（　　　　　　　　　　　　　）／（　　　　　　　　　　　　　）／（　　　　　　　　　　）(excerpt from a meeting)／（　　　　　　　　　　　　　）／（　　　　　　　　　　）(スーパーや劇場) などです。

Part 4の典型的なトークの流れは、「情報提供 → 次の行動」です。例えば以下のように大まかな流れが決まっています。

Part 3同様、設問も2パターンがあり、会話全体のテーマやトピックを尋ねる「（　　　）」問題と、1か所にしか出てこない詳細を尋ねる「（　　　）」問題がありました。よって、問題がどんな情報を聞き取る問題なのかを意識しておくのがポイントでした。

「全体」問題の設問文例：What is the purpose of this talk?

「詳細」問題の設問文例：When will the conference be held?

Part 4 ● トーク問題

ではトークを聞いて正しい答えをひとつ、選んでみましょう。

(51) **Questions 1 through 3 refer to the following excerpt from a speech.**

❶ Who most likely are the listeners?

(A) Instructors for a workshop

(B) Visitors to a library

(C) Reporters at a press conference

(D) Participants in a training Ⓐ Ⓑ Ⓒ Ⓓ

❷ What are the listeners asked to do?

(A) Leave the room　(B) Pick up some papers

(C) Write a report　(D) Review some invoices Ⓐ Ⓑ Ⓒ Ⓓ

❸ What will Ms. Clarkson probably do?

(A) Introduce a speaker　(B) Distribute course material

(C) Describe a recent event　(D) Discuss protection techniques Ⓐ Ⓑ Ⓒ Ⓓ

(52) **Questions 4 through 6 refer to the following advertisement.**

❹ What kind of business is Dino's?

(A) A hotel　(B) A restaurant

(C) An outdoor market　(D) A botanical garden Ⓐ Ⓑ Ⓒ Ⓓ

❺ According to the speaker, what has Dino's done recently?

(A) Open a restaurant　(B) Given a cooking demonstration

(C) Expanded the garden　(D) Organized a party Ⓐ Ⓑ Ⓒ Ⓓ

❻ What are listeners invited to do on Saturday?

(A) Have a special lunch　(B) Register for membership

(C) Learn some recipes　(D) Write reviews Ⓐ Ⓑ Ⓒ Ⓓ

(53) **Questions 7 through 9 refer to the following talk.**

❼ What is the main purpose of the talk?

(A) To introduce a speaker　(B) To review a project plan

(C) To demonstrate a product　(D) To recognize a staff member Ⓐ Ⓑ Ⓒ Ⓓ

❽ What field does Harry Walsh work in?

(A) Food service　(B) Software development

(C) Customer service　(D) Financial planning Ⓐ Ⓑ Ⓒ Ⓓ

❾ What is Harry Walsh known for?

(A) Owning a company　(B) Founding a school

(C) Writing a book　(D) Directing for a research center Ⓐ Ⓑ Ⓒ Ⓓ

Exercise Questions! 🚶🚶 >>>

以下は先のページの問題のスクリプトです。音声を聞いて空所に入る単語を書き取ってみましょう。また、先ページの問題が「全体」問題か「詳細」問題か識別してみましょう。出来たら、ペアで、グループで、同じかどうか確認してみましょう。

(51) **Questions 1 through 3 refer to the following excerpt from a speech.**

Now that our morning (　　　　) is coming to an end, please go to the table at the back of the room to pick up your training packet, which (　　　　) course materials, articles, and biographies of our (　　　　). Before we take a break, find a seat and take a minute to review the article of Ms. Clarkson, our first speaker. You'll need to learn to use special (　　　　) to protect documents from damage. We're fortunate to have an expert in the field. After the ten-minutes break, Ms. Clarkson will (　　　　) a session.

❶ (　　　　　　) ❷ (　　　　　　) ❸ (　　　　　　　　)

(52) **Questions 4 through 6 refer to the following advertisement.**

Do you enjoy eating healthy meals created with fresh (　　　　)? Then you should try Dino's, the restaurant (　　　)(　　　) serving garden fresh meals. When we first opened, our chef grew all the herbs we needed in a small kitchen garden. And now this year, we are (　　　　) the garden, to include (　)(　　　)(　　) vegetables, ensuring that we cook with fresh ingredients all year long. Dino's invites diners to a special lunch on Saturday. We'll use some of the new vegetables grown, including asparagus, tomato, and zucchini.

❹ (　　　　　　) ❺ (　　　　　　) ❻ (　　　　　　　　)

(53) **Questions 7 through 9 refer to the following talk.**

Good evening, everyone. My name is Sophie Williams. It's a great pleasure for me to introduce our (　　　　), Harry Walsh. He will talk about the three most common personal financial-planning mistakes. This is a subject in which we should all be deeply interested because it's by avoiding financial mistakes that we can best ensure our (　　　　) futures. Harry has spent almost his entire (　　　　) advising people on their finances in Chicago. He is an award-winning professional (　　　　) who has specialized in personal finances and taxation for over twenty years. He is also known for his best-selling book, *"Financial Future"*. Like you, I am looking (　　　) to hearing his pearls of wisdom. Ladies and gentlemen, Harry Walsh.

❼ (　　　　　　) ❽ (　　　　　　) ❾ (　　　　　　　　)

More Exercise Questions! 🚶 >>>

答え合わせが終わったら、リスニング力をあげるためにも音読の練習をたくさんしましょう。

Part 7にはUnit 3で学習したSP（　　　　　　　　　　　　　　）のほかにDP
（　　　　　　　　　　　　）と呼ばれる、文書が（　　）ある問題が出題されました。
このパターンは通例（　　　　）出題されて、Questions176-185に割り当てられ
ています。そして2つの文書に対し（　　）つの設問があり、2題で合計（　　）
問となります。文書が（　　）つになっても基本的なスタンス、1問1分は同じで
すので、DP 2題を（　　　）分で解き終わらせられることを目標にしましょう。

設問のタイプとしては

文書全体の主題、テーマを問う全体問題

> **例** ▶ What is the article about? / Why was the e-mail sent? /
> Why was the letter written?

文書の一部の詳細を問う個別問題

> **例** ▶ What information does Mr. A want? /
> Where does Mr. B work?

文書には書いていないことを問うNOT問題

> **例** ▶ What is NOT true about ...? /
> Who will NOT attend the meeting?

これらの問題に加え、同義語問題（文中の単語と同じ意味の単語を選ぶ問題）が加わりました。

文書が2つあったとしても、全ての問いに対して2つの文書を読まなければならない、どちらの内容
も把握していないと答えられない、ということは実はありません。むしろ、2つの文書を参照して内
容を確認しなければならない問題は5問中1, 2問で、残りの問題はSPと同じアプローチで解けます。

基本的に、最初の問題のヒントは最初のほうに、最後の問題のヒントは最後のほうにある場合が多い
です。

Part 7 ● 読解問題

ではPart 7 DPの問題を実際にやってみましょう。制限時間は5分です。

Questions 1-5 refer to the following advertisement and e-mail.

═ O'Kelly Virtual Theater ═

Our subscriptions bring you theater at your home. With no late seating issues, no worries
about silencing your cellphone, unlimited restroom breaks, and more.

Join us for a season of new live readings, a new fully-produced virtual musical direct from
the O'Kelly Theater stage, and monthly plays in the O'Kelly Theater on Alice Street.

As a subscriber, you can choose one of the four options below:

Virtual Only Subscription
Get all digital content for $20
- Valid for virtual content, excluding live readings
- Excludes in-person shows in our theater on Alice Street

Virtual + On Demand Subscription
Packages starting at $50
- Valid for all the virtual content
- Access to live and on-demand streaming options

Virtual + In-Person Subscription
Packages starting at $100
- Valid for virtual and in-person productions, excluding benefit readings
- Access to live and on-demand streaming options
- 2 complimentary tickets to each in-person production

Patron Membership
Membership from $ 300
- Access to all Virtual Programming
- 5 complimentary tickets to each in-person production
- Invitations to Patron events
- Personal concierge at Alice Street
- Tax-deductible

To:	Oliver Evans <oliverevans@mapmail.com>
From:	Jessica Brown <customerservice@virtualtheater.com >
Subject:	O'Kelly Virtual Theater
Date:	November 5

Hello, Mr. Evans.

Thank you for subscribing to O'Kelly Virtual Theater. We will be sending you content from our theater. We have been one of the leading companies for ten years, so you will be receiving only the best content. We hope you enjoy our on-demand streaming options and two tickets for monthly plays.

With our new automatic renewal policy, subscribers to O'Kelly Virtual Theater no longer have to worry about missing out on our entertainment services. Once your subscription has begun, it will continue without interruption unless you state otherwise. If we do not hear from you, the subscription will be renewed for another year, at the same rate, regardless of price changes.

If you have any questions or comments about the content you're receiving, please e-mail back and we will respond to your inquiry promptly.

Sincerely,

Jessica Brown
Customer Service Representative

❶ What is being advertised?

    (A) Tickets to an exhibition   (B) A classic concert

    (C) A subscription service   (D) A discount on a movie   Ⓐ Ⓑ Ⓒ Ⓓ

❷ Why did Ms. Brown e-mail Mr. Evans?

    (A) To show her gratitude

    (B) To advertise a new agricultural product

    (C) To inform him of a special promotion

    (D) To offer him a discount on a subscription   Ⓐ Ⓑ Ⓒ Ⓓ

❸ What is indicated about O'Kelly Virtual Theater?

    (A) It is currently offering a 20 percent discount to new subscribers.

    (B) It is attracting more subscribers than last year.

    (C) It has been in business for a decade.

    (D) It is a family-owned business.   Ⓐ Ⓑ Ⓒ Ⓓ

❹ In the e-mail, the word "promptly" in paragraph 3, line 2, is closest in meaning to

    (A) formerly   (B) swiftly   (C) increasingly   (D) suspiciously   Ⓐ Ⓑ Ⓒ Ⓓ

❺ Which plan did Mr. Evans most likely purchase?

    (A) Virtual Only Subscription   (B) Virtual + On-Demand Subscription

    (C) Virtual + In-Person Subscription   (D) Patron Membership   Ⓐ Ⓑ Ⓒ Ⓓ

Exercise Questions! 🚶

左ページでやったパート７の問題を分析してみましょう。どういうタイプの問題だったでしょうか。

❶(   ) ❷(   )

❸(   ) ❹(   )

❺(   )

More Exercise Questions! 🚶🚶

問題文を使って、今度はもう少し正確に読んでみましょう。ここでは線を引いたり、単語に丸をつけたりしてもかまいません。正解の根拠となる部分をしっかりつかみましょう。終わったら、ペアで、グループで、それらを確認してみましょう。なお、時間は先生の指示に従ってください。

↳ *Review for Today's Lesson*

What did you learn today?

では今日学んだことを自分の言葉でまとめておきましょう。
まとめられたらペアの人と確認してください。

■ リスニングについて

■ リーディングについて

■ 来週までにするべき課題、自分の目標

自分の目標をしっかりペアの人に宣言し終わりましょう。

Unit 14

Part 4-2 | Part 7 TP (Triple Passage)

 **Listening** ‥‥

> | グラフィック問題 意図問題 |

Unit 13ではPart 4のトーク問題の基本を復習しました。このUnitではPart 3にも出題されている形式、グラフィックと意図問題に取り組んでみましょう。

グラフィック問題はUnit 5でも取り上げましたが、会話を聞きながら問題冊子に印刷されている表や地図を参照し、その情報についての問いに答える問題です。なお、このタイプの問題はPart 4の最後の3セット (Questions 92-94, 95-97, 98-100) に登場し、グラフィック情報についての設問はそのセットの中に1問だけ (つまり3セットで合計3問) あります。また、その際は必ずLook at the graphic.というアナウンスが流れます。その他の2問 (3セットで6問) は通常のPart 4の問題と変わりはありません。

グラフィックの例：

Expense Report		
Description	**Description**	**Amount**
Date	Car Rental	$200
July 2	Restaurant	$30
July 10	Hotel	$150
July 21	Road Service	$50

意図問題とは、トークの中で使われた表現がどういう意図を示しているのか問う問題です。例えば、イベントの紹介がなされているトークで "How could you miss this?" (どうして見逃せるでしょうか？) と言われたら、その真の意図は「ぜひ参加してください」ということになります。このように、言葉の表面的な意味ではなく、言わんとしている意図を正確に把握する問題です。この問題の際には必ず、Why does the speaker say, "…"?、もしくはWhat does the speaker imply when he says, "…"?のような質問文が流れます。

> | Part 4 ● トーク問題 |

ではトークを聞いて正しい答えを選んでみましょう。

◉ グラフィック問題 ◉

(54) **Questions 1 through 3 refer to the following telephone message and schedule.**

Expense Report		
Date	**Description**	**Amount**
July 1	Car Rental	$200
July 2	Restaurant	$30
July 10	Hotel	$150
July 21	Road Service	$50

❶ In what department does the speaker work?

    (A) Sales

    (B) Research

    (C) Human Resources

    (D) Accounting

❷ Look at the graphic. Which receipt cannot be found?

(A) Car Rental   (B) Restaurant

(C) Hotel   (D) Road Service

Ⓐ Ⓑ Ⓒ Ⓓ

❸ What will the speaker most likely do next?

(A) Explain some procedure   (B) Contact a client

(C) Meet with a manager   (D) Schedule a meeting

Ⓐ Ⓑ Ⓒ Ⓓ

(55) **Questions 4 through 6 refer to the following telephone message and map.**

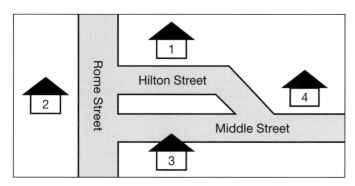

❹ Who most likely is the speaker?

(A) A real estate agent   (B) An apartment building manager

(C) A utility company employee   (D) A construction site supervisor

Ⓐ Ⓑ Ⓒ Ⓓ

❺ Look at the graphic. Which house does the listener want to know about?

(A) 1   (B) 2   (C) 3   (D) 4

Ⓐ Ⓑ Ⓒ Ⓓ

❻ What is the listener asked to do?

(A) Make a phone call   (B) Return a confirmed form

(C) Make a payment   (D) Confirm a reservation

Ⓐ Ⓑ Ⓒ Ⓓ

(56) **Questions 7 through 9 refer to the following excerpt from the meeting.**

❼ Why will the company have a dinner party?

(A) To entertain guests from overseas   (B) To compliment employees

(C) To welcome a new president   (D) To have an award ceremony

Ⓐ Ⓑ Ⓒ Ⓓ

❽ Why does the speaker say, "but some of you have other ideas"?

(A) To invite suggestions   (B) To discuss an award winner

(C) To confirm an estimate is correct   (D) To read customer reviews

Ⓐ Ⓑ Ⓒ Ⓓ

❾ What information does the speaker say she will e-mail to listeners.

(A) The date of the event   (B) A menu of a restaurant

(C) A time schedule   (D) A list of guests

Ⓐ Ⓑ Ⓒ Ⓓ

Exercise Questions! 🚶🚶 >>>

以下は先のページの問題のスクリプトです。音声を聞いて空所に入る単語を書き取ってみましょう。また、先ページの問題が「全体」問題か「詳細」問題か識別してみましょう。出来たら、ペアで、グループで、同じかどうか確認してみましょう。

(54) | **Questions 1 through 3 refer to the following telephone message and schedule.**

Hi, I'm Kelly Sanchez in Accounting. I'm working with your (　　　　) report, and I need some information (　　　　) your last business trip. Actually, I can't find one of your receipts. I haven't found the receipts on July 2. If you have the receipt, please send it to (　　　　) by in-house mail. If you don't have it, please (　　　　) me at 555-0166. I'll teach you how to process the expense without the receipt. Thanks.

❶ (　　　　　　　)　❷ (　　　　　　　)　❸ (　　　　　　　)

(55) | **Questions 4 through 6 refer to the following telephone message and map.**

Hello Ms. Fernando, this is America Miller from Saratoga Real Estate. I'm calling because you (　　　　) information about the house on Rome Street. I'm (　　　　) right now to answer questions. I found a couple of other homes near the one you're interested in, and they are similarly priced. Do you want to talk tonight? You can call or (　　　　) me at 555-7551. I look forward to (　　　　) with you and answering any questions. Again, my number is 555-7551. Thank you!

❹ (　　　　　　　)　❺ (　　　　　　　)　❻ (　　　　　　　)

(56) | **Questions 7 through 9 refer to the following excerpt from the meeting.**

Before we end the meeting, I'd like to (　　　　) a bit about our company's (　　　　). Our company will sponsor an all-paid company dinner for employees as a gesture of appreciation. I think Gary Danko will be the best place, but some of you have other ideas. It has a big party room, and the food is great. I think the restaurant is the (　　　　) location. If you have any other ideas, please (　　　　) me at ext. 23. I will e-mail all of you more details and the (　　　　) time schedule about the party. Thanks.

❼ (　　　　　　　)　❽ (　　　　　　　)　❾ (　　　　　　　)

Exercise Questions! 🚶 >>>

答え合わせが終わったらリスニング力をあげるためにも音読の練習をたくさんしましょう。基本的に、口に出して「言えない」ものは「聞き取れない」と言われています。何度も練習して、スピード、発音、共に問題の音声に近づけることが出来るよう練習しましょう。

More Exercise Questions! 🚶🚶 >>>

ペアの人に向かって、話しかけるようにスクリプトを読んでみましょう。それぞれの状況に応じて、雰囲気を出してみてください。

Reading ....

Part 7 TP
復習

Unit 7を参考に、空所に適切な数字や単語を入れて文を完成させましょう。

Part 7の最後の（　　）題、Questions186-200はTP（　　　　　　　　　　　）
と呼ばれる、文書が（　　）つあるパターンの読解問題です。（　　）つも文書が
あるので読むのが大変、かつ難しそう、という印象を持つかもしれませんが、文
書（　　）つを全部つなぎあわせないと答えられない問題は基本的にありません。

1. SPと同様に1つの文書を読めば解ける問題

2. A、B、Cの3つの文書があったとして、AB、BC、ACのいずれか（　　）つの文書
を参照すれば解ける問題

このいずれかのパターンで解けるということです。

5問中1,2問は、これまで同様SPと同じアプローチで解けます。加えて、最初の問題のヒントは最初のほ
うに、最後の問題のヒントは最後のほうにある場合が多いのもポイントです。

Unit 3でも書きましたが、600-700点を目指す人は、200番まで全て解く必要はありません。最後まで
解き終わらずに塗り絵（業界用語で適当に塗ること）をしても良いのです。ただし、だからといってTPのト
レーニングをしなくて良い、ということではありません。TPも含めて読解練習をやることで、だんだんスピー
ドがついてきます。

Part 7 ● 読解問題

ではPart 7のTPの問題を実際にやってみましょう。制限時間は5分です。

Questions 1-5 refer to the following product information, review and response.

■ Polestar Tablet Cases

Tablet Size	Price
20 cm	$34.00
25 cm	$40.00
30 cm	$46.00
One size fits all	$50.00

Product features: All Polestar tablet cases are made of durable plastic with rubberized corners for an almost drop-proof design. They have integrated stands to keep your tablet at an optimum viewing angle. Magnetic closure ensures ease of opening and closing. Three colors to choose from: black, tan, and blue. (customizing available for an extra $12)

Customer Review: ★★★
Polestar 30 cm tablet case

I have tried numerous tablet cases and the Polestar case is by far the best, most durable on the market. As a geologist, I travel extensively for work and use my tablet in rough terrain. I've dropped it on hard rocky surfaces more than once and the Polestar case is the only one that has protected it completely. An added bonus was having my company's logo stamped on it.

The only gripe I have is that the closure seems to have lost its strength so sometimes the cover flies open. Therefore, it gets three stars from me.

Eric Fredriksen

Hello Mr. Fredriksen,

Thank you for leaving a review of our product. I was sorry to hear of your trouble with your tablet case. Our designers would like to take a look at it to see what the problem is. Please send the case back to us and we will send a replacement case to you by overnight express. We understand that due to the demands of your job, you can't be without a case for long.

Madison Parker, Customer Support

❶ How much did Mr. Fredriksen pay to have his company logo stamped on his case?

(A) $10   (B) $12   (C) $34   (D) $40   Ⓐ Ⓑ Ⓒ Ⓓ

❷ What does Mr. Fredriksen like the most about his case?

(A) The color   (B) The corners   (C) The price   (D) The size   Ⓐ Ⓑ Ⓒ Ⓓ

❸ What does Mr. Fredriksen mention about his job?

(A) He enjoys his work.   (B) He needs up-to-date technology.
(C) He spends time outside.   (D) He works a lot of overtime.   Ⓐ Ⓑ Ⓒ Ⓓ

❹ What will Ms. Parker's company investigate?

(A) The logo stamp   (B) The magnetic closure
(C) The plastic material   (D) The stand   Ⓐ Ⓑ Ⓒ Ⓓ

❺ In the response, the word "see" in line 2, is closest in meaning to

(A) expect   (B) meet   (C) understand   (D) view   Ⓐ Ⓑ Ⓒ Ⓓ

Exercise Questions! 🚶 ⟫⟫⟫

左ページでやったパート7の問題を分析してみましょう。どういうタイプの問題だったでしょうか？

❶ (   ) **❷** (   ) **❸** (   )

❹ (   ) **❺** (   )

More Exercise Questions! 🚶🚶 ⟫⟫⟫

問題文を使って、今度はもう少し正確に読んでみましょう。ここでは線を引いたり、単語に丸をつけたりしてもかまいません。正解の根拠となる部分をしっかりつかみましょう。終わったら、ペアで、グループで、それらを確認してみましょう。なお、時間は先生の指示に従ってください。

⤷*Review for Today's Lesson*

What did you learn today?

では今日学んだことを自分の言葉でまとめておきましょう。

■ リスニングについて

■ リーディングについて

■ 来週までにするべき課題、自分の目標

ペアで（グループで）上に書いた内容を共有し、自分の目標をしっかり宣言しましょう。

Unit 15　クォーター模試 / 自己分析

クォーター模試（リスニング25問、リーディング25問）をやってみましょう。時間は30分間です。

問題は先生から配布されますのでそれを使ってください。マークシートはこの本の巻末にあります。

答え合わせをした後、どのパートが出来た／出来なかったのか、自己分析してみましょう。

● Part 1	（　　 / 2 ）	● Part 5	（　　 / 8 ）
● Part 2	（　　 / 8 ）	● Part 6	（　　 / 4 ）
● Part 3	（　　 / 9 ）	● Part 7	（　　 / 13 ）
● Part 4	（　　 / 6 ）		
● Listening	（　　 / 25 ）	● Reading	（　　 / 25 ）
● Total	（　　 / 50 ）		

出来たところ、出来なかったところを自分の言葉で以下にまとめてみましょう。

■ リスニング

_____

_____

_____

_____

_____

■ リーディング

_____

_____

_____

_____

_____

■ Unit 8の結果と比べてみましょう。どのパートがより出来るようになったでしょうか。

_____

_____

_____

_____

_____

■ 今後、学習したいポイント

_____

_____

_____

_____

_____

シートを書き終わったら、ペアで、グループで、その内容を共有して、自分の目標を宣言しましょう。

— **Unit 8** クォーター模試・解答用紙 —

Student ID:	Date:
Name:	Score: /50

Listening Part

Part 1

1	Ⓐ Ⓑ Ⓒ Ⓓ
2	Ⓐ Ⓑ Ⓒ Ⓓ

Part 2

3	Ⓐ Ⓑ Ⓒ
4	Ⓐ Ⓑ Ⓒ
5	Ⓐ Ⓑ Ⓒ
6	Ⓐ Ⓑ Ⓒ
7	Ⓐ Ⓑ Ⓒ
8	Ⓐ Ⓑ Ⓒ
9	Ⓐ Ⓑ Ⓒ
10	Ⓐ Ⓑ Ⓒ

Part 3

11	Ⓐ Ⓑ Ⓒ Ⓓ
12	Ⓐ Ⓑ Ⓒ Ⓓ
13	Ⓐ Ⓑ Ⓒ Ⓓ
14	Ⓐ Ⓑ Ⓒ Ⓓ
15	Ⓐ Ⓑ Ⓒ Ⓓ
16	Ⓐ Ⓑ Ⓒ Ⓓ
17	Ⓐ Ⓑ Ⓒ Ⓓ
18	Ⓐ Ⓑ Ⓒ Ⓓ
19	Ⓐ Ⓑ Ⓒ Ⓓ

Part 4

20	Ⓐ Ⓑ Ⓒ Ⓓ
21	Ⓐ Ⓑ Ⓒ Ⓓ
22	Ⓐ Ⓑ Ⓒ Ⓓ
23	Ⓐ Ⓑ Ⓒ Ⓓ
24	Ⓐ Ⓑ Ⓒ Ⓓ
25	Ⓐ Ⓑ Ⓒ Ⓓ

Reading Part

Part 5

26	Ⓐ Ⓑ Ⓒ Ⓓ
27	Ⓐ Ⓑ Ⓒ Ⓓ
28	Ⓐ Ⓑ Ⓒ Ⓓ
29	Ⓐ Ⓑ Ⓒ Ⓓ
30	Ⓐ Ⓑ Ⓒ Ⓓ
31	Ⓐ Ⓑ Ⓒ Ⓓ
32	Ⓐ Ⓑ Ⓒ Ⓓ
33	Ⓐ Ⓑ Ⓒ Ⓓ

Part 6

34	Ⓐ Ⓑ Ⓒ Ⓓ
35	Ⓐ Ⓑ Ⓒ Ⓓ
36	Ⓐ Ⓑ Ⓒ Ⓓ
37	Ⓐ Ⓑ Ⓒ Ⓓ

Part 7

38	Ⓐ Ⓑ Ⓒ Ⓓ
39	Ⓐ Ⓑ Ⓒ Ⓓ
40	Ⓐ Ⓑ Ⓒ Ⓓ
41	Ⓐ Ⓑ Ⓒ Ⓓ
42	Ⓐ Ⓑ Ⓒ Ⓓ
43	Ⓐ Ⓑ Ⓒ Ⓓ
44	Ⓐ Ⓑ Ⓒ Ⓓ
45	Ⓐ Ⓑ Ⓒ Ⓓ
46	Ⓐ Ⓑ Ⓒ Ⓓ
47	Ⓐ Ⓑ Ⓒ Ⓓ
48	Ⓐ Ⓑ Ⓒ Ⓓ
49	Ⓐ Ⓑ Ⓒ Ⓓ
50	Ⓐ Ⓑ Ⓒ Ⓓ

— **Unit 15** クォーター模試・解答用紙 —

Student ID:	Date:
Name:	Score: /50

Listening Part

Part 1
- 1　Ⓐ Ⓑ Ⓒ Ⓓ
- 2　Ⓐ Ⓑ Ⓒ Ⓓ

Part 2
- 3　Ⓐ Ⓑ Ⓒ
- 4　Ⓐ Ⓑ Ⓒ
- 5　Ⓐ Ⓑ Ⓒ
- 6　Ⓐ Ⓑ Ⓒ
- 7　Ⓐ Ⓑ Ⓒ
- 8　Ⓐ Ⓑ Ⓒ
- 9　Ⓐ Ⓑ Ⓒ
- 10　Ⓐ Ⓑ Ⓒ

Part 3
- 11　Ⓐ Ⓑ Ⓒ Ⓓ
- 12　Ⓐ Ⓑ Ⓒ Ⓓ
- 13　Ⓐ Ⓑ Ⓒ Ⓓ
- 14　Ⓐ Ⓑ Ⓒ Ⓓ
- 15　Ⓐ Ⓑ Ⓒ Ⓓ
- 16　Ⓐ Ⓑ Ⓒ Ⓓ
- 17　Ⓐ Ⓑ Ⓒ Ⓓ
- 18　Ⓐ Ⓑ Ⓒ Ⓓ
- 19　Ⓐ Ⓑ Ⓒ Ⓓ

Part 4
- 20　Ⓐ Ⓑ Ⓒ Ⓓ
- 21　Ⓐ Ⓑ Ⓒ Ⓓ
- 22　Ⓐ Ⓑ Ⓒ Ⓓ
- 23　Ⓐ Ⓑ Ⓒ Ⓓ
- 24　Ⓐ Ⓑ Ⓒ Ⓓ
- 25　Ⓐ Ⓑ Ⓒ Ⓓ

Reading Part

Part 5
- 26　Ⓐ Ⓑ Ⓒ Ⓓ
- 27　Ⓐ Ⓑ Ⓒ Ⓓ
- 28　Ⓐ Ⓑ Ⓒ Ⓓ
- 29　Ⓐ Ⓑ Ⓒ Ⓓ
- 30　Ⓐ Ⓑ Ⓒ Ⓓ
- 31　Ⓐ Ⓑ Ⓒ Ⓓ
- 32　Ⓐ Ⓑ Ⓒ Ⓓ
- 33　Ⓐ Ⓑ Ⓒ Ⓓ

Part 6
- 34　Ⓐ Ⓑ Ⓒ Ⓓ
- 35　Ⓐ Ⓑ Ⓒ Ⓓ
- 36　Ⓐ Ⓑ Ⓒ Ⓓ
- 37　Ⓐ Ⓑ Ⓒ Ⓓ

Part 7
- 38　Ⓐ Ⓑ Ⓒ Ⓓ
- 39　Ⓐ Ⓑ Ⓒ Ⓓ
- 40　Ⓐ Ⓑ Ⓒ Ⓓ
- 41　Ⓐ Ⓑ Ⓒ Ⓓ
- 42　Ⓐ Ⓑ Ⓒ Ⓓ
- 43　Ⓐ Ⓑ Ⓒ Ⓓ
- 44　Ⓐ Ⓑ Ⓒ Ⓓ
- 45　Ⓐ Ⓑ Ⓒ Ⓓ
- 46　Ⓐ Ⓑ Ⓒ Ⓓ
- 47　Ⓐ Ⓑ Ⓒ Ⓓ
- 48　Ⓐ Ⓑ Ⓒ Ⓓ
- 49　Ⓐ Ⓑ Ⓒ Ⓓ
- 50　Ⓐ Ⓑ Ⓒ Ⓓ

アクティブ・トレーニングで
スコアアップを目指す TOEIC® L&R テスト

| 検印省略 | ⓒ 2021 年 1 月 31 日　初版発行 |

編著者	関 戸　冬 彦
	長 田　いづみ
	西 嶋　愉 一
発行者	原　雅 久
発行所	株式会社　朝 日 出 版 社

101-0065　東京都千代田区西神田 3-3-5
電話　東京　03-3239-0271〜72
FAX　東京　03-3239-0479
e-mail　text-e@asahipress.com
振替口座　00140-2-46008
組版／イーズ　製版／錦明印刷

乱丁、落丁本はお取り替えいたします。
ISBN978-4-255-15668-2